# Introduction

The impetus of this study is ___ of passages that depict Jesus *'sitt___ ;ht hand of God.'* Many Christians ___ ice of this terminology; consequently, their interpretation of this Biblical motif often degenerates into ditheism or tritheism. This is unfortunate because such faulty explanations actually obscure the Biblical meaning of the phrase—causing one to miss the powerful message contained in the metaphor.

Oneness Pentecostals firmly acknowledge the validity of this phrase and its applicability to the work and ministry of the glorified Messiah—Jesus Christ. However, they reject any suggestion that *"the right hand of God"* is a *literal* or *tangible* place of spatial relationship—where *one distinct 'person of God'* is in literal proximity to another *'person of God'*. Rather, Oneness theology holds to a Hebraic understanding of this phrase—emphasizing Jesus' *mediatory* and *redemptive* role as high priest.

Oneness theologians are not alone in their hermeneutical treatment of this phrase; indeed, most Trinitarian scholars share the same view. Unfortunately, average believers (Oneness and Trinitarian) have difficulty explaining this Biblical concept due to their misunderstanding of the meaning and significance of the Biblical phase "the Right hand of God." It is our prayer that you will be enlightened through this study—walking away with a greater understanding of what the Bible means when it speaks of Jesus at God's right hand.

# Table of Contents

I. God's Nature and the Significance of the Right Hand..................................................................3

II. The Glorified Christ & the Mediatory Work at God's Right Hand........................................................17

III. The Mediatory Work of the 'Right Hand' UNTIL..................................................................35

IV. The Eschatological Abdication of the 'Right Hand'..................................................................49

V. From the Right Hand to the Center of the Throne..................................................................67

*Selected Bibliography*..................................................79

# I

# God's Nature & The Significance of the 'Right Hand'

In order to correctly comprehend the Biblical meaning of God's *'right hand'*—it is necessary to grasp the Scriptural revelation that God is an invisible, incorporeal Spirit.

> But the hour cometh and now is, when the true worshippers shall worship **the Father** in spirit and in truth: for **the Father** seeketh such to worship him. **God is a Spirit**: and they that worship him must worship him in spirit and in truth (John 4:23-24).

This passage affirms the essential nature of God is transcendent Spirit. Moreover, Jesus uses the familial term 'the Father' when referring to God, which is consistent with the way this word is used to denote the God of Israel in the Old Testament.

> Do ye thus requite **the LORD**, [יהוה]...Is not he thy father that hath bought thee? Hath he not made thee, and established thee? (Deuteronomy 32:6).
>
> ...Blessed by thou, **LORD** [יהוה] God of Israel our father, for ever and ever (1Chron 29:10).
>
> ...But now, O **LORD** [יהוה] art thou our father, our redeemer, thy name is from everlasting (Isaiah 63:16).
>
> But now, O **LORD** [יהוה] thou art our father...(Isaiah 64:8).

Notice carefully that the above citations employ the relational term "Father" in conjunction with the tetragrammaton. Thus, יהוה (Yahweh) the God of Israel is the one designated as the "Father." This is significant because it shows that—when used of God, 'Father' is a relational appellation or descriptive noun for the one true God—**NOT** an *eternally distinct hypostasis in the Godhead.*

According to John 4:24 the one true God and Father is 'spirit' (πνεῦμα) a word defined as:

> air in movement...that which animates or gives life to the body...an independent noncorporeal being, in contrast to a being that can be perceived by the physical senses.[1]
>
> πνεῦμα in Jn 4:24...is highly generic...the reference is simply to a supernatural and non-material entity.[2]

---

[1] Fredrick William Danker, πνεῦμα, in A Greek-English Lexicon of the New Testament and other Early Christian Literature. (BDAG) Third edition, (Chicago, IL: University of Chicago, 2000). Electronic edition.

[2] Johannes P. Louw and Eugene A. Nida, Editors, πνεῦμα in Greek-English Lexicon of the New Testament Based on Semantic Domains, (New York, NY: United Bible Societies, 1989), electronic edition.

The King James Version (KJV) renders John 4:24 "God is **a** Spirit;' yet, the Greek text literally says πνεῦμα ὁ θεός (*Spirit **the** God*).³ This is important because—if "God is Spirit" then He does **not** possess literal bodily appendages. This truth is reiterated in the Gospel of Luke.

> Behold my hands and my feet, that it is I myself: handle me, and see; for **a spirit hath not flesh and bones**, as ye see me have (Luke 24:39).

As 'Spirit,' God is not limited to the strictures of a physical body, but is omnipresent—simultaneously filling heaven and earth.

> Whither shall I go from thy spirit? or whither shall I flee from thy presence? If I **ascend up into heaven, thou art there**: if I make **my bed in hell, behold, thou art there**. If I take the wings of the morning, and dwell in the uttermost parts of the sea; Even there shall thy hand lead me, and thy right hand shall hold me (Psalm 139:7-10).

> But will God indeed dwell on the earth? behold, the **heaven and heaven of heavens cannot contain thee**; how much less this house that I have builded? (1Kings 8:27).

> Am I a God at hand, saith the LORD, and not a God afar off? Can any hide himself in secret places that I shall not see him? saith the LORD. **Do not I fill heaven and earth? saith the LORD** (Jeremiah 23:23-24).

In truth, the Bible argues against a portrait of God as a GIANT human occupying a particular dimension of space.

> ...we should not think of God as having size or dimensions even infinite ones...God does not have a physical body, nor is he made of any kind of matter...God's spirituality means that God exists as a being that is not made of any matter, has no parts or dimensions, is unable to be perceived by our bodily senses...⁴

The Biblical truth regarding God's *incorporeality and omnipresence* is further augmented by its teaching on God's **invisibility**.

> **No man hath seen God at any time**; the only begotten Son, which is in the bosom of the Father, he hath declared him (John 1:18).

---

³ Maurice A. Robinson and William G. Pierpont, The New Testament in the Original Greek: Byzantine Textform 2005, (GNT 2005) electronic edition. Unless otherwise stated this textform is used throughout.

⁴ Wayne Grudem, Systematic Theology, (Grand Rapids, MI: Zondervan, 1994), 188.

> **No man hath seen God at any time**. If we love one another, God dwelleth in us, and his love is perfected in us (1John 4:12).
>
> Who is the image of **the invisible God**, the firstborn of every creature: (Colossians 1:15).
>
> Now unto the King eternal, **immortal, invisible**, the only wise God, be honour and glory for ever and ever. Amen (1Timothy 1:17).
>
> Which in his times he shall shew, who is the blessed and only Potentate, the King of kings, and Lord of lords; Who only hath immortality, dwelling in the light which no man can approach unto; **whom no man hath seen, nor can see:** to whom be honour and power everlasting. Amen (1Timothy 6:15-16).

The word *'invisible'* (*i.e. Col. 1:15; 1Tim. 1:17*) is translated from the Greek word ἀόρατος, denoting *"...that which cannot be seen."*[5] Interestingly, in Colossians 1:15 the Apostle uses the Greek article (THE) before *God* and *invisible* (τοῦ θεοῦ τοῦ ἀοράτου) thus, the literal rendering is: *"of The God of The invisible."* Yet, if God is invisible—what is the meaning of passages indicating He has been 'seen'?

> The emphatic declaration, "No man hath seen God at any time..." is in line with #Ex 33.20...Yet there are some passages like #Ex 24.9-11 which explicitly affirm that some men have seen God...This passage is not meant to deny that men had witnessed "manifestations" of God, as when he appeared to Moses and the prophets (compare Num 12:8; Isa 6:1-13); but it is meant that no one has seen the essence of God...[6]

Some stumble at this truth because of the Old Testament verses that refer to visible manifestations of God (*ex. Burning bush, pillar of fire, 'glory' cloud, a man*). Yet, these are temporal appearances and **not** an incarnate embodiment. God never *became* a burning bush, or a pillar of fire of a literal human in the Old Testament. Therefore, such instances do not contradict the Scriptural truth of God's invisibility. Indeed, scholars refer to these as **theophanies** —*temporary visible manifestations of God.*

> God spoke to men through their senses, in physical phenomena, as the burning bush, the cloudy pillar, or in

---

[5] Louw & Nida, ἀόρατος.

[6] Larry Pierce, ed., Eclectic Notes on the Bible, electronic edition, Online Bible for Windows (OBW) (Ontario, Canada: Online Bible, 2003).

sensuous forms, as men, angels, etc...."[7]

These 'temporal' theophanies are not literal physical descriptors of God—but vehicles of God's self-disclosure designed to assist humans in their comprehension of the Divine.

God's <u>incorporeality</u> and <u>invisibility</u> are *fundamental* teachings of Scripture; thus, passages attributing <u>human,</u> <u>animal</u> or <u>fowl</u> appendages to God must be interpreted in light of these twin truths. Indeed, rather than a literal physical designations of God, such language is understood as an '<u>*anthropomorphism*</u>', which is a pedagogical literary device designed to explain the *infinite* and *incomprehensible* using *finite* and *comprehensible* terms.

> By this term is meant...as being in the form or likeness of man, the attribution to God of human form, parts or passions, and the taking of Scripture passages which speak of God as having hands, or eyes, or ears, in a literal sense. This anthropomorphic procedure called forth Divine rebuke as early as <u>Psa 50:21</u>: "Thou thoughtest that I was altogether such a one as thyself."[8]

Scriptural anthropomorphism was never viewed literally in normative Judaism or the early church. Rather, both recognized this to be a metaphoric means of revealing something about God that would otherwise be hidden or unknown. Sadly, many post-modern Christians fail to recognize the figurative nature of anthropomorphisms—insisting on a literal interpretation of such language. This often results in a portrait of God that is demeaning and obscures the <u>true</u> message of the pictorial metaphor.

In truth, the contradictory and ridiculous conclusions resulting from a literal interpretation of anthropomorphic language is the best argument **against** this interpretive model. For example:

> I will say of the LORD, He is my refuge and my fortress: my God; in him will I trust. He shall cover thee **with his feathers**, and **under his wings** shalt thou trust: his truth shall be thy shield and buckler (Psalm 91:2, 4).

> The LORD recompense thy work, and a full reward be given thee of the LORD God of Israel, under **whose wings** thou art come to trust (Ruth 2:12).

---

[7] Ibid., <u>International Standard Bible Encyclopedia</u>, <u>OBW</u>.

[8] James Lindsay, *"Anthropomorphism"* in <u>The International Standard Bible Encyclopedia</u>, internet site, <u>www.topicalbible.org</u>.

> Keep me as the apple of the eye, hide me under the shadow **of thy wing**...(Psalm 17:8).
>
> How excellent is thy lovingkindness, O God! therefore the children of men put their trust under the shadow **of thy wings** Psalm 36:7. [see also Psalm 57:1; 61:4; 63:7]

Clearly, if the metaphoric descriptions of God in the above verses are interpreted *literally*—then Yahweh possesses *feathers and wings*! Some may object by insisting a literal hermeneutic is to be applied **only** when the Bible uses 'human' features to describe God. Yet, there is **no** authoritative basis to support such an assertion. In fact, if the physical characteristics assigned to God are supposed to be viewed literally—this is true of **all** physical attributes—including **feathers and wings**!

In reality, the only way to properly interpret the above verses is to acknowledge the Bible's use of metaphoric anthropomorphism as a means of conveying a truth about God *transcending* the metaphor. Understood in this manner—*feathers* and *wings* are not literal physical attributes of God—but intentional metaphors that emphasize Yahweh's protection.

> Theologically, the key idea of God's protection occurs in Ps 91:4, where the psalmist uses the powerful imagery of a mother bird to speak of God who covers...with his feathers and spreads the protection of his wings over the righteous...[9]
>
> ...Yahweh's winged presence corresponds to the immediacy of divine action, the metaphor also elicits a trust in the comforting presence that offers protection from harm...Yahweh's protection is likened to the refuge a mother bird provides for its young.[10]

Other passages are equally absurd when one fails to recognize Scripture's use of metaphoric anthropomorphism. For example:

> Thus saith the LORD, **The heaven is my throne**, and the **earth is my footstool**: where is the house that ye build unto me? and where is the place of my rest? (Isaiah 66:1).

If metaphoric expression is disallowed—Isaiah 66:1 teaches heaven is a huge throne and Yahweh's 'feet' are *'resting'* on planet

---

[9] Willem A. VanGemeren, edt. New International Dictionary of Old Testament Theology & Exegesis, NIDOTTE, (Grand Rapids, MI: Zondervan, 1997) electronic edition.

[10] Ibid, George L. Klein and Gordon H. Matties כָּנָף.

earth. In fact, the Hebrew word '*footstool*' הֲדֹם is "*a piece of furniture on which one may rest one's feet.*"[11] No serious student of the Bible interprets this imagery literally. Rather, they understand Isaiah is using a literary metaphor to express God's sovereignty.

The fallacy of literally interpreting '*human*' descriptions of God is also readily apparent in the following verses.

> Then the magicians said unto Pharaoh, This is **the finger of God**: and Pharaoh's heart was hardened, and he hearkened not unto them; as the LORD had said (Exodus 8:19).
>
> And with the **blast of thy nostrils** the waters were gathered together, the floods stood upright as an heap, and the depths were congealed in the heart of the sea (Exodus 15:8).

The word 'finger' literally refers to a physical appendage; yet, no one believes Exodus 8:19 teaches that Pharaoh's magicians visibly 'saw' the tangible finger of God. Likewise, Exodus 15:18 uses the dual construction of 'nose' (*i.e. nostrils*)[12] to describe the parting of the Red Sea. Yet, no one imagines the parting of the waters were a result of Yahweh blowing **His nose**! Unfortunately, this is the only conclusion possible—if one subscribes to a literal view of physical attributes assigned to God!

In truth, most understand the '*finger of God*' as a reference to the power of God and that:

> "...the blast of your nostrils" is a bold anthropomorphic expression for the wind that came in a dried up the water.[13]

Perhaps the best way to avoid ridiculous, nonsensical conclusions regarding God's nature is to recognize the *emblematic* character of anthropomorphisms. In so doing, it is easy to see there are many verses of Scripture that express the *incomprehensible* attributes of God—using *comprehensible* metaphors.

> The **eyes of the LORD** are **in every place**, beholding the evil and the good (Proverbs 15:3).
>
> For **the eyes of the LORD run to and fro throughout the**

---

[11] Louw and Nida, ὑποπόδιον

[12] Ludwig Koehler and Walter Baumgartner, אַף in The Hebrew and Aramaic Lexicon of the Old Testament (HALOT) electronic edition, 2000.

[13] The NET Bible, first edition notes, *Exodus 15:8*, Biblical Studies Press, electronic edition, 2005.

**whole earth**, to shew himself strong in the behalf of them whose heart is perfect toward him…(2 Chronicles 16:9).

The Hebrew word translated '*eyes*' עַיִן (ain) refers to a "*…physical organ…of man…*"[14] Yet, neither of the above verses are suggesting God has literal pair of physical '<u>eyes</u>' **in** '*every place*' nor does He have a *pair of eyes* <u>running</u> around the earth. In fact, such an idea is ludicrous; yet, this is the conundrum faced by those who fail to grasp the figurative nature of anthropomorphic language.

Rather than resorting to the above skewed interpretations, it is more hermeneutically accurate to understand that Prov. 15:3 and 2Chron. 16:9 uses 'eyes' as a literary metaphor—communicating God's <u>omniscience</u> and <u>omnipresence</u>.

> Anthropomorphically eyes are attributed to God. His eyes are in every place observing the good and evil (Prov 15:3). They focus throughout the whole earth to defend the righteous (2 Chr 16:9)…[15]

It is important to remember there is no Biblical justification for teaching '*some*' anthropomorphic descriptions of God are 'literal,' while others are symbolic. Furthermore, the previous passages clearly show it is impossible to consistently interpret metaphoric anthropomorphic depictions of God in a **literal** manner—without violating the Biblical truth of God's <u>invisibility</u> and <u>incorporeality</u>.

Additionally, in some verses—a literal view of the text presents a comical image of God (*i.e. Ex. 15:8; 2Chron. 16:9*)—further illustrating the fallacy of literally interpreting <u>anthropomorphic-metaphoric language</u>. This does **not** mean one should abandon a literal hermeneutic when examining the Biblical text; indeed, this is the <u>preferred interpretive model</u>. However, when a literal view of a text places it <u>at variance</u> with other verses of Scripture, creates a <u>comical picture</u> of God or results in absurd conclusions—the literal hermeneutic is obviously **not** the proper method to be used in **that particular text.**

---

[14] Francis Brown, S.R. Driver and Charles A. Briggs, עַיִן, in <u>A Hebrew and English Lexicon of the Old Testament</u>, (BDB) electronic edition, Oak Tree Software.

[15] Charles Schulz, עַיִן, in <u>Theological Wordbook of the Old Testament</u>, (TWOT), (Chicago, IL: Moody, 1980), electronic edition.

Some are reticent to recognize *symbolism* or *metaphoric expressions* in Scripture—because liberals often use these literary features to attack the veracity of the Bible. Yet, acknowledging the use of anthropomorphisms is not a denial of Biblical authenticity nor does it detract from the reality of God's attributes. Rather, it clarifies the intent of the text and accentuates God's desire to communicate His infinite attributes to the human family.

This is especially evident when one examines the significance of one's hand in ancient Hebrew thought. Indeed, Scripture affirms the important symbolism of the *hand* and the primacy given to the *right hand*.

> The ancients made a careful distinction of the respective values of the two hands. This is perhaps best seen from Gen 48:13-19, where the imposition of the hands of aged Israel upon the heads of Joseph's sons seems unfair to their father, because the left hand is being placed upon the elder...[16]
>
> ..there was already a significance attached to the right hand...the idea of favor and strength being transmitted through the right hand of blessing begins to emerge...Benjamin "son of my right hand" clearly is a name showing special favor and position as the youngest son of Jacob.[17]

Scripture emphasizes the importance of one's hand and affirms the special status of the "right hand," as "...*the position of honor, privilege and preference...*"[18] (*i.e. 1Kings 2:19; Psa. 45:9*). Interestingly, the '*right hand*' is often used in reference to Yahweh (*i.e. Psalm 60:5; 63:8; 108:6; 118:15-16 etc...*). Since the Bible affirms that God is an invisible and incorporeal Spirit—He has **no** literal physical hands! Hence, when used of God—most scholars recognize the '*right hand*' as an anthropomorphic metaphor expressing power, glory, honor and preeminence.

> The more important usage for theological consideration is the figurative expression "the right hand of the Lord" which exhibits the omnipotence of God especially in behalf of his

---

[16] H. L. E. Lukring, "*Hand,*" i n Cambridge Comprehensive Bible Encyclopedia, online edition, 2011.
[17] R. Laird Harris, edt., יְמִינִי, TWOT. in Theological Wordbook of the Old Testament, electronic edition.
[18] VanGemeren, יְמִינִי, NIDOTTE.

people Israel.[19]

Several passages of Scripture confirm the metaphoric nature of the phrase *"right hand"* when applied to God. In fact, if interpreted literally—they are confusing and contradictory. For example:

> Thy **right hand**, O LORD, is become glorious in power: **thy right hand**, O LORD, hath **dashed in pieces the enemy**. Thou stretchedst out **thy right hand**, the earth swallowed them (Exodus 15: 6, 12).

The above passage clearly credits Yahweh's *'right hand'* with the defeat of the Egyptian army. Yet, Israel did **not** visibly witness the descent of God's tangible 'hand' when they crossed the Red Sea. Rather, the *"right hand"* imagery is used to graphically depict Yahweh's direct involvement in the deliverance of Israel!

> What is certain is that, like his arm, "the hand" and "right hand" of Yahweh are symbols of his power...this emphasizes the thought that God not only possesses incomparable power, but also exercises it...[20]

Understanding God's 'right hand' as an anthropomorphic metaphor does not devalue or diminish the significance of the *right hand* image, but it **does** argue against carnally interpreting Israel's redemption in terms of a giant *'human like'* hand!

> Though I walk in the midst of trouble, thou wilt revive me: thou shalt **stretch forth thine hand** against the wrath of mine enemies, and **thy right hand** shall save me (Psalm 138:7).

Like that of Exodus 15:6, 12—the Psalmist uses the metaphor of *'hand'* and *'right hand'* in the above Psalm to convey God's active involvement in his own life, providing protection and deliverance. This *redemptive language* is common in Scripture—and continues to be used by those who experientially encounter the delivering power of God. In fact, even among 21st century Pentecostals, it is not uncommon to hear testimonies of God's healing, salvation or deliverance using metaphors involving *'the hand of the Lord.'*

Interestingly, when a post-modern believer uses expressions like, *"I was touched by the hand of God,"* there is no confusion as to the meaning of the phrase. Indeed, rather than interpreting this as

---

[19] Harris, יְמִנִי, TWOT.

[20] VanGemeren, יְמִנִי, NIDOTTE.

literal reference to God's tangible appendage—the believer's use of *the hand of God* is understood as a symbolic metaphor describing their personal experience of God's power!

> That led them by the right hand of Moses with **his glorious arm**, *dividing the water* before them, to make himself an everlasting name? (Isaiah 63:12).

The above verse further accentuates the problems of literally interpreting metaphoric language. According to Isaiah 63:12, Yahweh's "***glorious arm***" is responsible for dividing the water of the Red Sea before the children of Israel. Yet, in Exodus 15:8, this event is accomplished by a '*blast*' of God's '*nostrils!*' If 'arm' and 'nostrils' are both interpreted as literal appendages—the verses are in conflict. However, if understood as distinct anthropomorphic metaphors emphasizing Yahweh's active role in delivering His people—both verses harmonize.

> ...The LORD came from Sinai, and rose up from Seir unto them; he shined forth from mount Paran, and he came with ten thousands of saints: from **his right hand went a fiery law** for them. Yea, he loved the people; all his saints **are in thy hand**: and they sat down **at thy feet**; every one shall receive of thy words (Deuteronomy 33:2-3).

This passage describes a **literal** theophanic event—using graphic imagery and metaphor. If interpreted literally—this passage is nonsensical and contradictory to other verses for it teaches that the Decalogue is a *"fire of a law, or fire was a law"*[21] proceeding from a physical '*hand.*' Of course, in reality—this passage of Scripture uses a dynamic metaphor to affirm the Divine origin of the Law.

> ...Under a beautiful metaphor, borrowed from the dawn and progressive splendor of the sun, the Majesty of God is sublimely described as a divine light which appeared in Sinai and scattered its beams on all the adjoining region in directing Israel's march to Canaan.[22]

Deuteronomy 33:2-3 also proclaims "*...all his saints are in thy hand.*" This verse may actually be the basis for the old Sunday School song *"He's got the whole world in His hand;"* yet, even little

---

[21] Brown et al., אש in BDB, electronic edition.
[22] Jamieson, Fausset, Brown, Critical and Explanatory Commentary on the Whole Bible, (JFB) online edition, www.biblestudytools.com.

children realize they are not *spatially located* in a giant *human-like appendage*. Thus, even those unfamiliar with metaphoric language intuitively recognize the intent of *this phrase* is to demonstrate that God guides and protects His children!

Scripture repeatedly uses the figurative metaphor of God's *hand* to express His power and preeminence. Yet, **at no time** is it used to teach God possesses a tangible appendage! Failing to recognize this truth leads to a false interpretation of Scripture and ultimately a distorted view of God.

> Thou wilt shew me the path of life: in thy presence is fulness of joy; at **thy right hand** there are pleasures for evermore (Psalm 16:11). [*If God's right hand is interpreted 'literally' then "<u>pleasures</u>" are a tangible reality spatially located at God's hand.*]
>
> Shew thy marvellous lovingkindness, O thou that savest **by thy right hand** them which put their trust in thee from those that rise up against them (Psalm 17:7).
>
> Thou hast also given me the shield of thy salvation: and **thy right hand hath holden me up**, and thy gentleness hath made me great (Psalm 18:35).
>
> Now know I that the LORD saveth his anointed; he will hear him from his holy heaven with the saving **strength of his right hand** (Psalm 20:6).
>
> For they got not the land in possession by their own sword, neither did their own arm save them: **but thy right hand, and thine arm**, and the light of thy countenance, because thou hadst a favour unto them (Psalm 44:3).
>
> According to thy name, O God, so is thy praise unto the ends of the earth: **thy right hand** is full of righteousness (Psalm 48:10).
>
> That thy beloved may be delivered; save with **thy right hand**, and hear me (Psalm 60:5).
>
> My soul followeth hard after thee: **thy right hand** upholdeth me (Psalm 63:8).
>
> [*There are at least 20 more verses—in the Psalms **alone**—that speak of God's right hand. In **every** instance the phrase is a metaphoric literary device and **never** indicative of a literal appendage.*]

Anthropomorphic references to God are problematic **only** when they are treated as literal physical realities. In truth, when one recognizes the purpose for using such theocentric metaphors is to reveal infinite characteristics in a manner easily grasped—faulty interpretations can be avoided. Thus, while *"arm"* and *"hand"* <u>can</u>

refer to a physical appendage—when used of God they are:

> ...an anthropomorphic figure of God's power. The most vivid of these instances occurs in Isa 30:30 in which the lightning stroke is pictured as the "descending blow of this arm."[23]

Scripture often refers to the hand or arm of God but *in neither Testament*, are they used as physical descriptors of God. Rather, these are theocentric metaphors that accentuate Yahweh's active role in the salvific deliverance of His people!

> Fear thou not; for I am with thee: be not dismayed; for I am thy God: I will strengthen thee; yea, I will help thee; yea, I will uphold thee with **the right hand** of my righteousness (Isaiah 41:10).
>
> Mine **hand** also hath laid the foundation of the earth, and **my right hand** hath spanned the heavens: when I call unto them, they stand up together (Isaiah 48:13).
>
> The LORD hath sworn **by his right hand,** and by **the arm of his strength,** Surely I will no more give thy corn to be meat for thine enemies; and the sons of the stranger shall not drink thy wine, for the which thou hast laboured: (Isaiah 62:8).
>
> Thou art filled with shame for glory...the cup of the **LORD'S right hand** shall be turned unto thee, and shameful spewing shall be on thy glory. (Habakkuk 2:16).

---

[23] Walter Kaiser, אֱזְרוֹעַ, in <u>TWOT</u>.

# II

# The Glorified Christ & The Mediatory Work at God's *Right Hand*

The Bible often uses <u>anthropomorphisms</u> when describing God's attributes or characteristics; yet, this language is not meant to be interpreted literally. Rather, this is a <u>metaphoric literary device</u> designed to aid individuals in their comprehension of God by using finite expressions to explain the infinite. Thus, when Scripture speaks of God's *'feet' 'feathers' 'wings' 'finger' 'face' 'hinder parts' 'eyes' 'nose'* or *'hand,'* this is not meant to convey the idea that the *invisible, incorporeal* God possesses <u>tangible bodily parts</u>. Rather, the Bible is expressing God's incomprehensible attributes in a manner humans can easily grasp.

In order to properly interpret such language, it is essential to understand the meaning of literary forms in the Scripture.

> ...the language of the Bible is God's means of communicating... it is the source of truth because it refers to God as the ultimate source of reality. However, as a means of communication it requires interpretation of the genres (story, law, genealogy, poetry, etc.) and of the literary forms (simile, metaphor).[24]

The Old Testament's use of metaphoric expressions comes as no surprise given the pictorial nature of the Hebrew language.

> Metaphor has long been considered the master image or even the essence of poetry...they lend richness of meaning to the poem and seek to evoke a strong emotional response from the reader.[25]

The previous chapter addressed the special significance given to the metaphoric expression concerning God's *'arm'* or *'right hand'* in the Old Testament. Like other physical attributes ascribed to God, the use of these words do **not** literally refer to a Divine physical appendage but denote Yahweh's saving, healing and delivering power! Interestingly, use of the anthropomorphic "<u>right hand of God</u>" is not limited to the Old Testament but is also found several times in the New Testament with specific reference to Jesus Christ.

The remainder of this study focuses on the question: *"What is the meaning of Biblical passages associating Jesus with the **right hand** of God?'* The answer to this question is: **revealed** through <u>messianic</u>

---

[24] VanGemeren, *Introduction*, <u>NIDOTTE</u>.

[25] Tremper Longman III, *'Literary Approaches and Interpretation*, in <u>NIDOTTE</u>.

prophecy; **realized** in the Messiah's redemptive-mediatory work of salvation and **culminates** in the eternal eschaton. In fact, the prophet Isaiah is the first to link the revelation of the Messiah with the arm of Yahweh.

> Therefore **my** people shall know **my name**: therefore they shall know in that day that I am he that doth speak: behold it is I. The LORD hath **made bare his holy arm** in the eyes of all the nations; and all the ends of the earth **shall see** the salvation of **our God**. (Isaiah 52: 6,10).

Most scholars agree Isaiah 52-53 are prophecies concerning the coming Messiah. Indeed, in this section *"...the correspondence with the life and death of Jesus Christ is so minute that it could not have resulted from conjecture or accident."*[26] The above verses are especially significant, in that, they declare the Messiah is the revealer of Yahweh's name and the *visible baring* of *"...**his holy arm**."* Moreover, according to the tenth verse—the revelation of Yahweh's arm is equated with the *visible appearance of Yahweh's salvation in the eyes of **all** nations!*

The Hebrew verb *'made bare'* is חשׂף chasaph—meaning *"to strip, strip off, lay bare, make bare, draw out."*[27] In Isaiah 52:10—this word is a *Perfect Tense verb* and normally expresses the idea of *'completed action'* but this form is often used in prophetic utterances because:

> Sometimes in Hebrew, future events are conceived so vividly and so realistically that they are regarded as having virtually taken place and are described by the perfect.[28]

Isaiah 52:10 is a graphic metaphor:

> ...taken from warriors, who made bare the arm for battle; and the sense is, that God had come to the rescue of his people as a warrior, and that his interpositions would be seen and recognized and acknowledged by all the nations...[29]

Old Testament scholars Keil and Delitzsh concur, noting that:

> ...As a warrior is accustomed to make bare his right arm up to the shoulder, that he may fight without encumbrance...so has

---

[26] JFB, *Isaiah 52:13*, electronic edition.
[27] חשׂף in BDB.
[28] James Strong, Strong's Hebrew and Chaldee Dictionary of the Old Testament, electronic edition, Oak Tree Software Inc.
[29] Albert Barnes, Notes on the Bible, electronic edition.

> Jehovah made bare His holy arm...[30]

No one believes Isaiah 52:10 teaches that Yahweh would roll up his sleeve to visibly reveal a <u>*giant physical arm*</u>! Rather, most realize this prophecy employs a powerful metaphoric anthropomorphism to emphasize Yahweh's active involvement in the redemption of humanity. Yet, recognizing the Biblical use of metaphor in this verse does not diminish the Scriptural truth that <u>all nations</u> would visibly apprehend Yahweh's salvation <u>*in*</u> and <u>*through*</u> the Messiah!

Isaiah 52:6-15 prophetically anticipates the incarnation using a powerful metaphor vividly revealing the Messiah's dual identity as both <u>human</u> and <u>divine</u>. Indeed, verses 13-14 stress the <u>genuine humanity</u> of the Messiah—while the 6th and 10th verses identify Him as the **<u>visible</u> manifestation** of Yahweh's arm. In short, Isaiah 52:6,10 expressly teaches all nations will experientially encounter Yahweh's redemption through the <u>visible revelation of His arm</u> in the person and name of the coming Messiah.

Isaiah's prophetic declaration is a beautiful depiction of God's involvement in the redemptive process. Indeed, <u>*in*</u> and <u>*through*</u> the Messiah—Yahweh takes on an additional manner of existence as a human—*incarnate*—while simultaneously continuing to exist as transcendent Spirit. Thus, the Messiah is ***<u>genuinely human</u>***, but not ***<u>exclusively human</u>***—He is Yahweh's salvific arm visibly manifest for the redemption of humanity. Yet, *"If the Messiah is identified as the visible revelation of Yahweh's arm—why does Scripture speak of the Messiah as **sitting** or **standing** on the "<u>**right hand of God**</u>?"*

The answer to this question is discovered by recognizing Isaiah 52:10 is a **<u>pre-incarnate</u>** prophecy of the **<u>incarnation</u>**. In contrast, every verse depicting the Messiah at God's *"right hand"* addresses a **<u>post-incarnate</u>** state that is linked to the redemptive-mediatory work of the *glorified Messiah* culminating in the eternal eschaton. When these truths are held in 'tension,' one will discover there is no incongruity between Isaiah's declaration and the work of the glorified Messiah at the *'right hand of God.'*

---

[30] C. F. Keil and F. Delitzsch, *Isaiah* in <u>Commentary on the Old Testament</u>, vol. 7 (Peabody, MA: reprint 1996), 497.

So then after the Lord had spoken unto them, he was received up into heaven, and **sat on the right hand of God** (Mark 16:19).

Hereafter shall the Son of man sit **on the right hand** of **the power of God** (Luke 22:69).

Therefore being **by the right hand of God** exalted, and having received of the Father the promise of the Holy Ghost, he hath shed forth this, which ye now see and hear (Acts 2:33).

Him hath God exalted **with his right hand** to be a Prince and a Saviour, for to give repentance to Israel, and forgiveness of sins (Acts 5:31).

But he, being full of the Holy Ghost, looked up steadfastly into heaven, and saw the glory of God, and Jesus **standing on the right hand of God** (Acts 7:55).

And said, Behold, I see the heavens opened, and the Son of man **standing on the right hand of God** (Acts 7:56).

Who is he that condemneth? It is Christ that died, yea rather, that is risen again, who is even **at the right hand of God**, who also maketh intercession for us. (Romans 8:34).

If ye then be risen with Christ, seek those things which are above, where Christ **sitteth on the right hand of** God (Colossians 3:1).

But this man, after he had offered one sacrifice for sins for ever, **sat down on the right hand of God** (Hebrews 10:12).

Looking unto Jesus the author and finisher of our faith; who for the joy that was set before him endured the cross, despising the shame, and is **set down at the right hand of the throne of God** (Hebrews 12:2).

Who is gone into heaven, and is **on the right hand of God**; angels and authorities and powers being made subject unto him (1Peter 3:22).

It is paramount to note that **every verse** depicting Jesus at God's *right hand* refers to the position occupied by *__the man, Christ Jesus__ subsequent* to his glorification and ascension. Thus, the *right hand of God* is **not** an ontological state but a *soteriological-eschatological* position assumed by the resurrected Christ in *time* **not** *eternity*. Thus, when the Bible speaks of Jesus at God's *'right hand,'* this is **not** a description of two eternal hypostatic distinctions of God in spatial relationship to each other. Rather, this is an eschatological designation strictly related to the salvific work of the resurrected Messiah.

In truth, the only way to avoid Scriptural contradiction when interpreting passages referring to Jesus '*on*' or '*at*' God's right hand—is to be guided by the previously established truths:

1. Scripture teaches God is an invisible, omnipresent, incorporeal Sprit who cannot be visibly apprehended outside of the incarnation (Col. 1:15; Heb 1:1,2; John 14:1-10).

2. The Bible *intentionally* uses anthropomorphic language to describe God to effectively communicate *infinite* attributes or characteristics to *finite beings*. Thus, such language must be viewed as metaphoric and figurative rather than literal.

The above dual premise—coupled with a proper view of Biblical monotheism precludes a ditheistic view of God's *right hand* that imagines two distinct entities in physical spatial relationship. This hermeneutic ignores the metaphoric Hebraism inherent in the phrase '*right hand of God*' and violates Scripture by suggesting there are two *human-like* bodies occupying heaven's throne room. Most importantly—this interpretation places Scripture at variance with Scripture—thus, it must be deemed false!

Clearly, a proper interpretation of Scripture **must** be governed by the Biblical text and **not** the post-apostolic ideological concepts placed upon the text. In fact, *a key* for determining the validity of any Biblical interpretation is revealed by its Scriptural *consistency*.

> The infallible rule of interpretation of Scripture is the Scripture itself...Scripture itself is the best context for interpreting Scripture. In modernity and postmodernity alike, however, interpreters have tended to provide Scripture with extrabiblical interpretive contexts.[31]

This interpretive 'rule' is critical when addressing such concepts as Jesus' position <u>at</u> or <u>on</u> '*the right hand of God.*' Indeed, the Biblical doctrines of monotheism, God's invisibility-incorporeality and the metaphoric use of '*right hand*' places **strictures** on the interpretive possibilities one can assign to this phrase. In the Old Testament, God's '*hand*,' '*arm*' or '*right hand*' is predominately a metaphor for Yahweh's salvific-delivering power. This is especially evident when used as a prophetic reference to the coming Messiah—who is explicitly identified as the revelation of Yahweh's arm that is visibly manifest for human redemption.

Like the Old Testament—the New Testament uses the literary

---

[31] Kevin Vanhoozer, "*Language, Literature, Hermeneutics and Biblical Theology*, in NIDOTTE.

metaphor of the *'right hand'* to express honor, exaltation, power, glory and preeminence. This is clearly seen in Jesus' statement to the high priest during his trial.

> Hereafter shall the Son of man sit **on the right hand of the power** of God (Luke 22:69).
>
> Jesus saith unto him, Thou hast said: nevertheless I say unto you, Hereafter shall ye see the Son of man **sitting on the right hand of power**, and coming in the clouds of heaven (Matthew 26:64).
>
> And Jesus said, I am: and ye shall see the Son of man **sitting on the right hand of power**, and coming in the clouds of heaven (Mark 14:62).

Interestingly, the above passages use the phrase *'right hand of power* and *'right hand of the power of God.'* This is problematic for those who insist on interpreting *'right hand'* literally because each verse affirms 'power' has a 'right hand.' Of course, most realize the word 'power' is an attribute used as a metaphoric circumlocution for God in each of these verses! Thus, right hand of God and right hand of power are equivalent phrases describing the *'position'* of power and preeminence afforded the resurrected, glorified Christ. In truth, all statements referring to God's **'right'**:

> ...are to be understood in this figurative sense, and not of a fixed and definite place in the highest of heavens.[32]

Most importantly, when God's 'right hand' is used in connection with Jesus—it never denotes one hypostasis of God in spatial relationship to another hypostasis of God. Rather, it is **exclusively** linked to the **resurrected and glorified human Messiah**. Thus, it is a metaphoric phrase affirming that the man, Christ Jesus has been elevated to a position *no other human being has attained!*

In addition to expressing power, preeminence and the exaltation of the glorified Messiah—the *'right hand'* is a *legal* term associated with the mediatory work of the priesthood. This is confirmed in both the Old and New Testament.

> The LORD said unto my Lord, Sit thou at my right hand, until I make thine enemies thy footstool. The LORD hath sworn, and will not repent, Thou art a priest for ever after the order of

---

[32] Joseph Henry Thayer, δεξιός, in Thayer's Greek-English Lexicon of the New Testament, electronic edition, Oak Tree Software.

Melchizedek (Psalm 110:1, 4).

This Psalm of enthronement will be examined in chapter three, but is introduced here simply to show the Messianic *'right hand'* is expressly associated with the office of the priesthood.

This truth is echoed by the writer of Hebrews who explicitly connects the placement of the glorified Messiah on the *'right hand'* with His mediatory work as high priest of the New Covenant.

> Now of the things which we have spoken this is the sum: We have such **an high priest**, who is **set on the right hand of the throne** of the Majesty in the heavens; (Hebrews 8:1).

This verse is significant because Hebrews 8:1-13 compares and contrasts the work of the Levitical priests and the priestly work of the *glorified* Christ (Heb. 8:1-13). This further proves *'right hand' (of God, of power, of the throne)* is not a literal 'spatial' location but a reference to the ongoing mediatory work of the Messiah.

The eighth chapter of Hebrews emphasizes the abolishment of the physical priesthood in lieu of the spiritual mediatory work of the glorified Messianic high priest. Thus, even though the words ἐκάθισεν ἐν δεξιᾷ in Hebrews 8:1 literally mean *'he sat in (on) right'* this is "**an idiom**..*an expression of assigning special importance or hight status to such an individual.*"[33] Furthermore, scholars agree that the *'right hand of God'* does not denote a literal spatial location.

> The exalted position which our great High Priest now occupies should commend both His person and His office in our esteem... Who is "set" or "seated": #Ac 7:55 **warns us** against interpreting this in **a carnal or literal manner**.[34]
>
> ...when it is said that Christ is at the right hand of God, the meaning is, that he is exalted to the highest honor in the universe...Of course **the language is figurative**-as God **has no hands literally**...[35]

Interestingly, Hebrews 8:1 reveals that *mediation* is a component of the *'right hand'* position. This is significant considering the Bible teaches the ongoing *__work of mediation__* is accomplished by the

---

[33] Louw & Nida, καθίζω ἐν δεξιᾷ, emphasis mine.

[34] Arthur W. Pink, An Exposition of Hebrews, vol. 1, online edition (Jay P. Green, 2002), 429.

[35] Barnes, *Hebrews*, in Notes on the Bible.

glorified Christ—**not** an *'eternal hypostasis'* in God. Unfortunately, mediation <u>in the Divine</u> is often misunderstood and misconstrued by sincere believers—further exacerbating the false interpretation of the *right hand of God.*

Many carnally perceive mediation within the Godhead as <u>two eternally distinct persons</u> in spatial proximity—one of whom pleads in behalf of believers to the other. This view of mediation is erroneous because it promotes ditheism (two gods) or denies the Divinity of one of the eternal persons (typically the one 'pleading). Of course, this inaccurate depiction can be avoided by examining the Apostle Paul's treatment of Divine mediation.

> For there is **one God,** and **one mediator** between God and men, **the man Christ Jesus**; (1Timothy 2:5).

Notice carefully, the Apostle Paul begins by declaring εἷς γὰρ θεός *(for {there is} one God).* The Greek εἷς is *"a cardinal numeral,"*[36] referring to *"a single person or thing, with focus on quantitative aspect..."*[37] This is significant because Paul is speaking of the **one** Deity (God)—**not** a hypostasis *o f* o r *in* the Deity. He continues with the words: εἷς καὶ μεσίτης θεοῦ καὶ ἀνθρώπων *(and one mediator of God and humans).* Just as there is <u>one</u> God—there is <u>one</u> mediator between the **one God** and humanity; thus, accentuating that the work of mediation has nothing to do with hypostases of God but that of <u>Deity</u> and <u>humanity</u>!

The word <u>mediator</u> is μεσίτης, which means *"one who mediates between two parties to remove a disagreement or reach a common goal..."*[38] 1Tim. 2:5 does **not** support the idea of mediation between *two hypostases* in the Godhead; yet, it **does** teach ***two parties*** are involved in the mediatory process—<u>Deity</u> and <u>humanity</u>. Indeed, Paul identifies the *mediated* a s <u>θεός</u> (God) and explicitly reveals the *mediator* is <u>ἄνθρωπος χριστὸς ιησοῦς</u> *(the man Christ Jesus).*

1Timothy 2:5 provides critical insight regarding the mediatory component of the *'right hand position.'* Rather than supporting the

---

[36] Thayer, εἷς, <u>Thayer's Greek-English Lexicon.</u>
[37] Danker, εἷς.
[38] Danker, μεσίτης.

unbiblical picture of mediation between two eternal persons of the Godhead—this passage clearly teaches mediation occurs in and through the glorified human in whom God resides, the man, Christ Jesus!

> Jesus Christ was incarnated; and being God and man, both God and men met in and were reconciled by him. But this reconciliation required a sacrifice on the part of the peacemaker or mediator...[39]

The Apostle Paul provides additional insight into the subject of Divine mediation in the Epistle of Galatians.

> Now a mediator is not a mediator of one, **but God is one**. (Galatians 3:20).

The Greek text begins with: Ὁ δὲ μεσίτης ἑνὸς οὐκ ἔστιν (*but the mediator is not of one*). This clearly affirms a mediator *presupposes two distinct parties*. Yet, the word μεσίτης (mediator) also indicates the intermediary belongs to both parties![40]

> ...Christ as the mediator, placing him in the middle as an intermediary between God and humans, the sole valid representative of **both parties**...[41]

Perhaps this is why Paul immediately follows this with the declarative statement ὁ δὲ θεὸς (but *the God*) εἷς ἐστίν (*one is*). Like 1Timothy 2:5—the Apostle Paul uses the numeral one in reference to God, but also includes the article before God; thus, emphasizing that he is speaking of THE God. Of course, this raises the question:

> *"How can mediation occur between two parties with the mediator belonging to both parties if **God is numerically one** and the mediator a genuine **human**?"*

This query is answered by recognizing the *two parties* involved in the mediatory process—*Divinity* and *Humanity*—are **localized** *in the person of Jesus Christ*. In short, Divine mediation is effected **in** and **through** the *one person* who is **simultaneously** God and man, the resurrected and glorified Savior—Jesus Christ.

---

[39] Adam Clarke, *1Timothy 2:5*, in Adam Clarke Commentary, online edition, www.studylight.org.

[40] Thayer, μεσίτης.

[41] Ceslas Spicq, μεσίτης, in Theological Lexicon of the New Testament, Hendrickson, 1994, electronic edition. Oak Tree Software.

> Now a mediator...must be of two parties...but God is one not two...not admitting of an intervening party...but as the ONE Sovereign, His own representative...For Jesus is not a mediator separating the two parties...but ONE in both nature and office with both God and man...bearing in Him "all the fullness of the Godhead..."[42]

Divine mediation does **not** require two *eternal hypostases*, but it **does** demand the mediator concurrently exist as the one true God and as a genuine human. This is impossible to visualize; however, one must remember that:

> ...in Jesus Christ, God did not send a substitute or a surrogate, no angelic mediation, no merely human go-between. In Jesus Christ, God, the one and only God, came himself.[43]

The prophet Zechariah affirms the dual identity of the Messianic Branch as king and priest saying that he:

> ...shall sit and **rule upon his throne**; and he shall be **a priest upon his throne**: and the counsel of peace shall be **between them both** (Zechariah 6:13).

The prophetic oracle of Zechariah 6:12-13 stresses the genuine humanity and Deity of the Messiah.[44] Indeed, there is little debate that Zechariah's 'Branch' is identified as both a *priest* and *king*. Yet, the most interesting phrase is that the counsel of peace "*shall be between them both.*" Since the Bible precludes the idea that a human can counsel as an equal with God (*Isa. 40:13-14*) many believe '*both*' does not refer to the human Branch and Yahweh but "*to the Moshel and Kohen (ruler and priest) who sit upon the throne united in one person, in the Tsemach*"[45]

The use of "both" in Zechariah's oracle is not speaking of *two persons in the Godhead* or *two abstract offices*. Rather, like the Apostle Paul's treatment this prophetic witness affirms that *both Divinity* and *Humanity* are **localized** in the person of the BRANCH! Thus, the mediatory counsel resulting in peace between Yahweh and the

---

[42] Jamieson, Fausset, Brown, *Galatians 3:20*.

[43] Timothy George, Galatians, in The New American Commentary vol. 30 (Broadman & Holman, 1994), 258.

[44] A more extensive treatment of this passage is provided in this author's work The Revelatory Name of God.

[45] Keil and Delitzsch, *Zechariah 6*, electronic edition, 300. The underlined words were aded by this author for clarification.

human family is wrought in and through the *one person* who is simultaneously *human* and *Divine*—the Messiah!

One of the most convincing proofs that the priestly work of the mediatory *"right hand"* is not a reference to one *eternal hypostasis* pleading the 'case' of a believer to another *eternal hypostasis* is found in the Scriptural portrayal of the heavenly **'throne.'**

> In the year that king Uzziah died I saw also the Lord sitting upon **a throne**, high and lifted up, and his train filled the temple...mine eyes have seen the King, **the LORD** (YHWH) of hosts. (Isaiah 6:1, 5).
>
> And above the firmament that was over their heads was the likeness of **a throne** as the appearance of a sapphire stone: and upon the likeness of **the throne** was the likeness as the appearance of **a man** upon it (Ezek. 1:26).

In both visionary experiences—Isaiah and Ezekiel are given a glimpse into the heavenly throne room. There are three features within these verses that confirm the metaphoric nature of the '*right hand*' and reject the idea of eternal hypostases in God. First, in the English, Hebrew and Septuagint translation of these verses, the word *"throne"* is **singular**; thus, emphasizing there is only **one throne**. Second, in both verses Yahweh—the God of Israel—is visibly represented as a **singular personage** seated on the throne.

Thirdly, Ezekiel describes the personage as the "*likeness as the appearance of a man.*" The Hebrew word 'likeness' is a rendering of דְּמוּת *(demooth)* while 'appearance' is translated from that of מַרְאֶה *(mareh).*[46] The former, דְּמוּת *(demooth)* expresses the idea of *"likeness, similitude, of external appearance...something that appeared like,"*[47] while מַרְאֶה *(mareh)* "*normally refers to the outward appearance...in the sense of how someone appears to be*"[48] Thus, the juxtaposition of these words indicates Ezekiel did **not** see a genuine human, but what *seemed* to be a singular personage resembling a man.[49]

---

[46] Adrian Schenker edt., Ezekiel 1:26, in Biblia Hebraica Stuttgartensia, (BHS)., 4th Edt., (Stuttgart, Germany, Deutsche Bibelgesellschaft, 1983) electronic format, 'The Groves Center,' 2010.

[47] Brown, Driver, Briggs, דְּמוּת.

[48] Jackie A. Naude, מַרְאֶה, in New International Dictionary of Old Testament Theology & Exegesis.

[49] Victor Hamilton, דְּמוּת, in Theological Wordbook of the Old Testament.

The prophetic picture of the heavenly throne room is confirmed in the New Testament.

> And immediately I was in the spirit: and, behold, **a throne** was set in heaven, and one sat on **the throne** (Revelation 4:2).
>
> And there shall be no more curse: but **the throne** of God and of the Lamb shall be in it; and **his** servants shall serve **him** and they shall see **his face**; and **his name** shall be in their foreheads (Revelation 22:3-4).

Like Isaiah and Ezekiel—the Apostle John uses the singular θρόνος (throne) to emphasize there is only **one**. The throne is identified as *"the throne of God and of the Lamb;"* yet, there is only **one personage** visibly seated thereon. This is explicitly revealed by John's use of the singular masculine participle—καθήμενος (*lit. he or the one seated*) in Revelation 4:2 and the *four singular pronouns (him & his)* in Revelation 22:3-4.[50]

The eschatological glimpse of the heavenly throne in Revelation 22:3-4 further confirms the priestly work of Divine mediation is accomplished **in** the <u>one person of Jesus Christ</u>. Indeed, the only one seated on ὁ θρόνος τοῦ θεοῦ καὶ τοῦ ἀρνίου (*"the throne of God and of the lamb"*) is the Alpha and Omega—the *one who is <u>human</u> and <u>divine</u>—God incarnate in the glorified man, Christ Jesus (see Rev. 21:5-7; 22:1-7, 12-13).* There is simply nothing suggesting there are two eternal hypostases sitting side by side in eternity.

The New Testament uses the *'right hand of God'* like that of the Old Testament—yet, it also uses it specifically with reference to mediatory work of the glorified man, Christ Jesus. Regrettably, some disregard the many verses affirming the metaphoric nature of *'the right hand of God'* and insist this is a literal place of spatial relationship. In fact, some argue Acts 7:55 supports this view, arguing when Stephen looked into heaven *"...two were side by side and <u>both were seen</u> by the natural eyes..."*[51]

---

The twenty-seventh verse confirms this is not a genuine human being.

[50] Robinson, *Revelation 4:2; 22:3-4*, <u>GNT 2005</u>. The KJV affirms this using four singular pronouns in Revelation 22:3-4.

[51] Finis Jennings Dake, *Acts 7:55*, in <u>Dake's Annotated Reference Bible</u>, (Lawrenceville, GA, 1961). Of course, if *"both"* are <u>seen</u> and *"both"* are God—there are two gods, which is ridiculous.

> But he, being full of the Holy Ghost, looked up steadfastly into heaven, and saw **the glory of God**, and Jesus **standing on the right hand of God** (Acts 7:55).

The above text clearly describes Stephen's experience in terms of a *visible apprehension*. However, it does **not** teach Stephen saw *two distinct beings in spatial relationship*. In fact, most Bible scholars reject this view because it places *Scripture at variance with Scripture*; thus, violating a major premise of sound hermeneutics. First, this view conflicts with the Scriptural doctrine of God's invisibility by teaching Stephen 'saw' the one *"...no man hath seen, nor can see..."* (1Tim 6:16).

Second, this view denies the truth of God's incorporeality (John 4:24) by teaching 'God' has a visible body distinct from Jesus; thus, contradicting **every other passage** that uses the metaphor of God's *'right hand'*! Finally, this position *plunders the Divinity* of Jesus by making him **something other than God**! Indeed, Acts 7:55 does **not** indicate Stephen beheld Jesus on the *'right hand'* of a *hypostasis of God* (i.e. the Father). Rather, the text literally says Jesus is standing on the *'right hand'* of τοῦ θεου (*'The God'*).[52] In short, Luke intentionally uses the definite article (**THE**) before God—to emphasize he is referring to *"...the only and true God: with the article."*[53] Thus, if Stephen saw *two personages*—Jesus is someone other than **THE** God!

Any interpretation of Acts 7:55 suggesting Stephen 'saw' two visible beings contradicts Biblical Monotheism. Indeed, this means either: there are two visible Gods (Ditheism) or Jesus is something less than THE God (Arianism). Actually, Luke's use of the *'right hand'* metaphor in Acts 7:55 is consistent with the way he utilizes it in other verses (*i.e. Luke 22:69; Acts 2:33; 5:31*). Clearly, Luke uses the phrase as a descriptive metaphor stressing the preeminence and power of the glorified **human** Messiah. The same is true of its use in Acts 7:55-56; in fact, careful examination of this text reveals Stephen saw ***only one personage*** when he looked up into heaven.

---

[52] Robinson, *Acts 7:55*, GNT 2005.
[53] Thayer, θεός. Emphasis mine.

According to Acts 7:55, Stephen looked up into heaven and saw δόξαν θεοῦ (<u>glory of God</u>) καὶ Ἰησοῦν ἑστῶτα (*and* <u>Jesus standing</u>). The <u>only way</u> this can denote *two spatially distinct visible entities* is if Scripture teaches the *'glory of God'* is a circumlocution for <u>one eternal hypostasis in the Godhead (i.e. the first person)</u>. Yet, neither Testament uses the *'glory of God'* to designate a distinct 'person' of the Godhead. Rather, this phrase is used with reference to the visible manifestation often accompanying the presence of God. Indeed, the Hebrew word rendered 'glory' כָּבוֹד is:

> ...etymologically, power, authority and honour of God; however it is often connected with manifestations of light.[54]
>
> כָּבוֹד as a technical term for God's manifest presence. The normal use of the expression כְּבֹד יהוה, the glory of the Lord... Here we can see two recurring associations כָּבוֹד is something seen...and it is tied to the cloud...[55]

The Old Testament describes the visible manifestation of God's glory in a variety of ways (*i.e. cloud, smoke, fire, light*) in several passages of Scripture.

> And the **glory of the LORD** abode upon mount Sinai, and <u>the cloud</u> covered it six days: and the seventh day he called unto Moses out of <u>the midst of the cloud</u>. And the sight of the **glory of the LORD** was like <u>devouring fire</u>...(Exodus 24:16-17).
>
> Then <u>a cloud</u> covered the tent...and the **glory of the LORD** filled the tabernacle. And Moses was not able to enter into the tent...because <u>the cloud</u> abode thereon, and the **glory of the LORD** filled the tabernacle (Exodus 40:34-35).
>
> And the posts of the door moved at the voice of him that cried, and the house was filled <u>with smoke</u> (Isaiah 6:4).
>
> And, behold, **the glory of the God of Israel** came from the way of the east: and his voice was like a noise of <u>many waters</u>: and the <u>earth shined</u> with his glory (Ezekiel 43:2).

In the New Testament—the word *'glory'* is from the Greek δόξα, which—like its Hebrew counterpart—expresses:

> the condition of being bright or shining, brightness, splendor, radiance (a distinctive aspect of Hebrew כָּבוֹד).[56]
>
> It translates most often the Hebrew *kabod*...This is how biblical

---

[54] Ludwig Koehler and Walter Baumgartner, כָּבוֹד.

[55] C. John Collins, כָּבוֹד in <u>NIDOTTE</u>.

[56] Danker, δόξα.

*doxa,* the manifestation of the presence and activity of the invisible transcendent God answers to sense experience: even though its brilliance cannot be perceived by the eyes of flesh.[57]

Interestingly, the New Testament also uses 'glory' in reference to the visible manifestation of God's presence.

> And the temple was filled <u>with smoke</u> from the **glory of God**, and from his power...(Revelation 15:8).
>
> ...And shewed me that great city, the holy Jerusalem, descending out of heaven from God, having the **glory of God**: and her <u>light</u> was like unto a stone most precious, even <u>like a jasper stone, clear as crystal</u>; (Revelation 21:10-11).
>
> And, lo, the angel of the Lord came upon them, and **the glory of the Lord** <u>shone</u> round about them...(Luke 2:9).

Perhaps the greatest difference between the Old and New Testament use of '*glory*' is the later ***visibly localizes*** *God's glory* in the person and name of Jesus Christ.

> For God, who commanded the <u>light to shine</u> out of darkness, hath <u>shined</u> in our hearts, to give <u>the light</u> of the knowledge of **the glory of God** in the face of Jesus Christ (2Corinthians 4:6).

The localization and emanation of God's 'glory' from the person of Jesus is most evident in the Transfiguration. In fact, Luke's account of this event specifically uses the term '<u>glory</u>' (Luke 9:31)!

Neither Matthew nor Mark uses '<u>glory</u>' in their Transfiguration narrative; yet, they use language expressly linked to the 'kabod' (glory) of God in the Old Testament (*i.e. the bright light and cloud enveloping the disciples—see., Matt. 17:2-8; Mark 9:2-8; Luke 9:28-36*). Of further interest—the Synoptics do not interpret the <u>bright light</u> or <u>the cloud</u> as a distinct hypostasis of God. Indeed, they clearly understand the visible and audible phenomenon as God's witness to the supreme object of worship—the one **in** whom HE resides, the man, Christ Jesus; thus, when they "*...lifted up their eyes, they saw no man,* **save Jesus only**" (Matthew 17:8).

Based on the Scriptural use of the "*glory of the Lord*" or "*glory of God,*" Stephen did not 'see' *two distinct hypostases of God.* Rather, he '<u>saw</u>' the <u>glory of God</u> "*the visible glory which surrounds and*

---

[57] Spicq, δόξὰ.

*proclaims God's near presence*"[58] Indeed:
> ...This phrase is commonly used to denote the visible symbols of God. It means some magnificent representation; a splendour, or light, that is the appropriate exhibition of the presence of God...[59]

Stephen's vision of God's glory (*i.e., smoke, cloud, light*) emanated <u>out from</u> and <u>around</u> the resurrected '*Son of man*,' a title stressing the genuine humanity of the glorified Christ who now occupies the '*right hand*' place of preeminence. Acts 7:55-56 describes the exalted position of the resurrected Christ as: ἑστῶτα ἐκ δεξιῶν τοῦ θεοῦ (*lit. 'standing out from the right of THE God'*). Of course, there is little debate that the Scriptural references to Jesus 'standing' or 'sitting' on the right hand is an idiom or "*expression of assigning special importance or high status to such an individual.*"[60]

As hitherto stated—a literal view of this text teaches that Jesus is *something other than* <u>The God</u>—contradicting both Trinitarian and Oneness views of God. Most importantly, this view conflicts with other verses of Scripture affirming Jesus is the God of the Bible. Indeed, John 20:28 records Thomas' confession identifying Jesus as **Ὁ κύριός** μου (<u>The Lord</u> of me) καὶ (and) **ὁ θεός** μου (<u>The God</u> of me).[61] Of course, the greatest testimony that Stephen did **not** see two personages is seen in his dying moments as he petitions the **only personage mentioned** in the text—the Lord Jesus Christ!

> And they stoned Stephen, calling upon the Lord, **and saying,** <u>Lord Jesus, receive my spirit</u>. (Acts 7:59 ASV).

When Scripture is '*rightly divided*' (*2 Tim. 2:15*) it is evident that the '*right hand of God*' is **not** a literal place of spatial relationship. Both Testaments use the phrase as an anthropomorphic metaphor denoting God's power. Yet, when used of Jesus—the phrase **also** denotes the *redemptive-mediatory work of the glorified human messiah*.

Most Trinitarians agree that '*the right hand of God*' is not referring

---

[58] A.C. Hervey, *Acts 7:55*, <u>Acts & Romans.</u>, Vol. 18, in <u>The Pulpit Commentary</u>, (Mclean, VA: McDonald Pub), 221.
[59] Barnes, *Acts 7:55-56*, <u>Notes on the Bible.</u>
[60] Louw & Nida, καθιζω ἐν δεξιᾷ.
[61] Robinson, *John 20:28*, <u>GNT</u> with English interlinear.

to a bodily appendage or a literal physical location; indeed:

> The apostles knew...they were using figurative language when they spoke of Christ's exaltation in these terms: they no more thought of a location...at God's literal right hand than their twentieth-century successors do...[62]

> Naturally, the expression 'right hand of God' cannot be taken literally, but should be understood as a figurative indication of the place of power and glory.[63]

> We are not to suppose that God has hands, or that Jesus sits in any particular direction from God. This phrase...means that he was exalted to honor and power in the heavens...[64]

---

[62] F. F. Bruce, The Epistles to the Colossians to Philemon, and to the Ephesians, The New International Commentary on the New Testament, (Grand Rapids, MI: Eerdmans, 1984), 132-133.

[63] Louis Berkhof, *The States of Christ*, Summary of Christian Doctrine, electronic edition.

[64] Barnes, *Mark 16* in Notes on the New Testament, electronic edition.

# III

# The Mediatory Work of the 'Right Hand'
## *UNTIL*

One of the most compelling proofs that the Christological use of *'the right hand of God'* does **not** refer to an eternal *physical location* is the <u>temporal nature</u> of the position. Indeed, every verse depicting Jesus '*at*' or '*on*' *the right hand of God* refers to the post-resurrected, glorified Messiah in His <u>mediatory capacity</u> as high priest. This is significant, for it demonstrates Jesus' exaltation to the *'right hand'* has a *<u>point of origin</u>*. Yet, Scripture also reveals Jesus' session at the *'right hand'* has a *<u>point of 'relative' termination</u>*.

> The **LORD** said unto <u>my Lord</u>, Sit thou *at my right hand*, **until** I make thine enemies thy footstool. The LORD hath sworn, and will not repent, Thou art **a priest** for ever after the order of Melchizedek (Psalm 110:1, 4).

The New Testament writers believed this *'Enthronement Psalm'* was Messianic—hence they quote and apply it to Jesus more than any other Old Testament text![65] The Psalm was *<u>partially realized</u>* in the glorification and ascension of Jesus—yet, its *<u>final culmination</u>* awaits the eternal eschaton. Unfortunately, there are some who have misconstrued the meaning and intent of the text—suggesting it depicts an actual *'heavenly'* dialogue between *eternal hypostases of God*. However, in reality, the Psalm employs:

> ...distinctively prophetic language, "the LORD says..." foresees a king greater than himself...this king will be a warrior king-priest after the order of Melchizedek.[66]

This is substantiated by the words נְאֻם יהוה *(Yahweh says)*. Most scholars recognize this is a '<u>prophetic formula</u>' because נְאֻם (says) is coupled with the divine name (i.e. יהוה) indicating an *"utterance, declaration of (the prophet citing divine word given through him)"*[67]

> This root is used exclusively of divine speaking. Hence, its appearance calls special attention to the origin and authority of what is said...Our noun occurs **only as a formula** (accompanied by the subject) declaring the divine...origin and authority of the message..."[68]

---

[65] Craig C. Broyles, *The Redeeming King: Psalm 72's Contribution to the Messianic Ideal*, in <u>Studies in the Dead Sea Scrolls and Related Literature</u>, (Grand Rapids, MI: Eerdmans, 2005), electronic edition. According to Broyles, this Psalm is quoted 25 times in the Greek New Testament.

[66] Bruce K. Waltke, *Psalms*, in <u>NIDOTTE</u>.

[67] Brown, Driver, Briggs, נְאֻם.

The Gospels of Matthew and Mark confirm the prophetic nature of Psalm 110:1-4—and explicitly reveal that Jesus did **not** interpret it as an *intra-dialogue between two eternal hypostases (i.e. the eternal Father and eternal Son)*. Rather, they demonstrate Jesus understood this to be a *prophetic utterance of David given by the Spirit*.

> He saith unto them, How then **doth David in spirit** call him Lord saying, (Matthew 22:43).
>
> For David **himself** said **by the Holy Ghost**, The LORD said to my Lord, Sit thou on my right hand, till I make thine enemies thy footstool (Mark 12:36).

Jesus' belief that Psalm 110:1 is a prophetic Davidic utterance is even more pronounced in the Greek text. Indeed, Matthew 22:43 says of David "κύριον αὐτὸν καλεῖ" (*lit., "**he calls** him Lord"*) and Mark 12:36 concurs saying, "Αὐτὸς γὰρ Δαυὶδ εἶπεν" (*for **David himself he said**). Obviously Jesus did not view Psalm 110:1-4 as a written record of a *heavenly dialogue* between 'two persons of the Godhead.' Thus, there is no justification for interpolating such a meaning into the text!

In truth, Jesus understood the Psalm as a prophetic utterance of David—written under the unction of the Spirit! According to Matthew 22:43—Jesus says David speaks ἐν πνεύματι (*in spirit*) and Mark 12:36 states, ἐν πνεύματι ἁγίῳ λέγει (*in the Holy Spirit he says*). Both Gospels use the preposition ἐν to describe the inspired utterance. The primary emphasis of ἐν is *localization—within—*yet, some believe in the above verses it designates:

> ...a close personal relation in which the referent of the ἐν-term is viewed as the controlling influence: *under the control of, under the influence of, in close association with*...to express the idea that someone is under the special influence of a good or even undesirable spirit: Mt 22:43; Mk 12:36...[69]

An honest examination of Scripture reveals there is no grounds for interpreting Psalm 110:1 in terms of an *intra-divine dialogue of eternal hypostases*. Rather, this prophecy is linked to the mediatory role of the glorified human Messiah—In fact, the:

---

[68] Harris, נאם.

[69] Danker, ἐν. This usage is also evident in the writings of John and Paul.

...explicit application of this Psalm to our Savior, by Him...and by the apostles (Act 2:34; 1Co 15:25; Heb 1:13)...leave no doubt of its purely prophetic character...The Psalm celebrates the exaltation of Christ...and a perpetual priesthood (Zec 6:13) involving the subjugation of His enemies...[70]

When Psalm 110:1-4 is properly categorized as '*prophetic speech*' it is clear this passage is intricately related to the mediatory work of the glorified human Messiah. Actually, the opening words נְאֻם יהוה לַאדֹנִי; *(Yahweh says to my Lord)* indicates this is **not** a conversation of 'persons' in the Godhead. This is evident considering the Divine name יהוה (Yahweh) is juxtaposed to the noun אדֹנִי (adona 'Lord') which is affixed with the pronominal suffix י ('my').

> Pronominal suffixes attached to nouns function as genitives, much like absolute nouns in construct relationships. In pronominal constructions however, the noun is said to be in the pronominal state and the suffix is normally a possessive pronoun.[71]

It is important to grasp the significance of the pronominal suffix to fully appreciate its bearing on the text. For example: the Hebrew word בֵּן *(ben)* is rendered 'son' in English; yet, "*my son*" or literally "*the son of me*" is formed by adding the *pronominal suffix* י to the Hebrew word 'son' בְּנִי *(i.e. Gen. 21:10)*.[72] The resultant meaning, is either *the son* 'from me' or 'belonging to me'. David's use of "*my Lord*" (lit. "*Lord of me*") in Psalm 110:1 follows the same pattern; thus, 'Is *David referring to the Lord who comes* '*from him*' or the Lord '*belonging to him*'? Of course, the Biblical answer is....YES!

Scripture demonstrates that David recognized no other 'God' or 'Lord' that *belonged to him* outside Yahweh—the God of Israel.

> O LORD (YHWH) our Lord אדֹנֵ (Adonay) how excellent is thy name in all the earth! Who hast set thy glory above the heavens (Ps. 8:1).
>
> O LORD (YHWH) our Lord אדֹנֵ (Adonay) how excellent is thy name in all the earth! (Ps. 8:9).

---

[70] Jamieson, Fausset and Brown, *Psalm CX*.
[71] Allen P. Ross, *Pronominal Suffix*, Introducing Biblical Hebrew, electronic edition, 2001. Emphasis mine.
[72] Paul Jouon, S.J. & T. Muraoka, *Pronominal Suffix*, in A Grammar of Biblical Hebrew, (Rome, Italy: Editrice Pontifico Istituto Biblico, 2006) electronic edition.

O my soul, thou has said unto the LORD (YHWH), Thou art my Lord אדני (Adonay)...(Ps. 16:2).

This thou hast seen, O LORD (YHWH): keep not silence: O Lord אדני (Adonay) be not far from me (Ps. 35:22).

Forsake me not, O LORD (YHWH): O my God, be not far from me. Make hast to help me, O Lord אדני (Adonay) my salvation (Ps. 38:21-22).

In each of the above verses—יהוה (Yahweh) is identified as אדני (Adonay)—a word denoting:

> ...one who has rule or authority; one of high rank; one who has dominion; one who is the owner or possessor, etc. This word is applied frequently to a creature...[73]

David consistently identifies Yahweh **AS** Adonay; yet, in Psalm 110:1 he juxtaposes the memorial name יהוה (YHWH) with the title אדני (Adonay); thus, drawing a distinction between the two.

Actually, there is **no** conflict between David's identification of Yahweh **as** Adonay and the distinction he makes in Psalm 110:1; in fact, **both are equally true**! This is especially clear considering Psalm 110:1-4 is a Messianic prophecy referring to the exaltation and mediatory work of the glorified Messiah—**who is both God and man**! Thus, the differentiation between *'The LORD' (Yahweh) and 'my Lord' (Adonay)* does **not** pertain to eternal hypostases—but to Yahweh and the glorified Christ—in whom YHWH is resident!

Confusion over Psalm 110:1-4 is eliminated by realizing this prophetic utterance is *incarnational* NOT *ontological*. David speaks *in and through the Spirit* concerning אדני (my Adonay)—the 'Lord' who **belongs** to me; **[and]** the 'Lord' who **comes from** me. Thus, his use of אדני (my Adonay) emphasizes that the coming one is **both** his **'offspring'** (Messiah) and his **'root'** or source (Yahweh). Thus, He **is** simultaneously a *descendent* of David and the only 'Lord' David recognizes—Yahweh.

A proper view of Psalm 110:1-4 is achieved when one adopts a hermeneutic recognizing this prophecy speaks of the incarnation and glorification of the human Messiah. It is a poetic portrayal of the exaltation of one who is **simultaneously** God and man to the

---

[73] Barnes, 151. Emphasis mine.

mediatory place of power—*the right hand of God*. Thus, David's use of אֲדֹנִי (my Adonay) is not a reference to distinct hypostases '*in the Godhead*' but stresses the **dual identity** of the Messiah as Yahweh incarnate. This is substantiated by Jesus in his discussion with the Pharisees.

> While the Pharisees were gathered together, Jesus asked them, saying, What think ye of Christ? whose son is he? They say unto him *The Son of David*. He saith unto them, How then doth David in spirit call him Lord, saying, The LORD said unto my Lord, Sit thou on my right hand, till I make thine enemies thy footstool? If David then call him Lord, how is he his son? (Matthew 22:41-45).

This passage gives an important interpretive stricture affirming the prophetic nature of Psalm 110:1-4 **and** the metaphoric use of '*right hand*.' It is significant that Jesus frames his citation of Psalm 110:1 around the question: *"What think ye of Christ?"* The meaning of 'Christ' (χριστός) is '*one who is anointed*', and it is the Greek equivalent of the Hebrew word rendered '*Messiah*.'[74] Like messiah—the appellation Christ (χριστός) is **not** a title of divinity, but refers to the "*fulfiller of Israelite expectation of a deliverer, the Anointed One, the Messiah...*"[75] In fact, Jesus' use of this word is a testimony to the messianic hope of Second-Temple Judaism.

> Towards the end of the Old Testament period, eschatological hope was sometimes linked with the expectation of a Messiah ("anointed one"), who would usher in the promised new age.[76]

The Messianic expectancy in Second Temple Judaism was rooted in several Old Testament themes—one of the most predominate being the Messiah's genealogical link to David. This is evident in the early church's consistent use of '*royal Psalms*' (i.e. Psalm 110:1-4) emphasizing Jesus as the promised Davidic Son.

> ...in the Hebrew Bible, notions about the Messiah are encapsulated in the figure of a royal Davidic king...Zechariah (6:9-15, esp. v. 13) refers to a high priest, along with a Davidic king.[77]

---

[74] Louw & Nida, χριστός.

[75] Danker, χριστός.

[76] Craig A. Evans and Peter W Flint, *Introduction for Eschatology, Messianism and the Dead Sea Scrolls*, in Studies in the Dead Sea Scrolls.

> The notion of "Messiah" or "Anointed One" is based largely, though not entirely, on the model of the anointed kings of the Davidic dynasty and the traditions associated with it...if we wish to focus on the royal paradigm...the obvious place to begin is the so-called "royal psalms" of the Hebrew Bible.[78]

It is important to reiterate that Scripture **never** uses '*Messiah*' or '*Christ*,' as a title of Divinity <u>to the **exclusion** of *genuine humanity*</u>! In other words, like the title "*Son of God,*" the Bible's designation of Jesus as *Messiah* or *Christ* is integrally tied to the incarnation and **never** denotes an eternal *hypostatic distinction in the Godhead*. Thus, the fact Jesus prefaces his citation of Psalm 110:1 with a question concerning the identity of "Christ" shows he interpreted Psalm 110:1 in the context of the incarnation.

Jesus' use of 'Christ' in Matthew 22:41-45 was consistent with Hebrew expectations that the Messiah would be a *genuine human descendent of David*. Yet, Jesus confounds the Pharisees—*not by suggesting Messiah is **one** hypostasis of God*—but by emphasizing the **dual identity** of the 'Christ' as simultaneously <u>God</u> and <u>man</u>!

> The scribes all taught the Messiah was to be the son of David (John 7:41)...the deity and the humanity of the Messiah are both involved in the problem. <u>Mat 22:45</u> [sic] observes that "no one was able to answer him a word.[79]

Psalm 110:1-4 teaches the Messiah is <u>*Creator*</u> and <u>*creature*</u>; <u>*LORD*</u> and <u>*Lord*</u>; <u>*mediator*</u> and <u>*Mediated*</u>. Yet, something often overlooked in this Psalm is the inclusion of a <u>*time constraint*</u> *[until]* regarding his occupation at the *mediatory right hand place*. This constraint is revealed in the Hebrew text by the particle עַד (ʿad) which is used as a *conjunction* and *preposition*—meaning: "*until...until a (certain time)...,*"[80] Employed as a noun—the word signifies eternity—but used as a prepositional particle (*i.e., Psa. 110:1*)[81]—it is "*properly, a*

---

[77] Paul E. Hughes, "*Moses' Birth Story: A Biblical Matrix for Prophetic Messianism,*" in <u>Studies in the Dead Sea Scrolls</u>.

[78] Craig C. Broyles, "*The Redeeming King...*"

[79] A. T. Robertson, *Mark 12:35*, in <u>Robertson's Word Pictures</u>, online edition, <u>www.bibletools.org</u>. Matt. 22:45 should be Matt. 22:46.

[80] Koehler and Baumgartner, עַד.

[81] Groves-Wheeler, *Psalm 110:1*, <u>Westminster Hebrew Morphology</u>, electronic edition.

*(peremptory) terminus...duration"*[82]

> The force of עַד is often pregnant, e.g. Jdg 19:26 "Then came the woman in the dawning of the day, and fell down at the door...till it was light," namely "she fell down and remained there till..."[83]
>
> עַד functions as both preposition and conjunction...it is used spatially, temporally and comparatively...This word is used temporally to indicate a continuation of an event from a point in the past to the present...also of an event in the future.[84]

The Septuagint translation of Psalm 110:1 substantiates this view using the Greek particle ἕως,[85] which denotes *"...the end of a period of time, till, until."*[86]

> a particle marking a limit...the temporal terminus...where something is spoken of which continued up to a certain time.[87]

Additionally, the New Testament citations of Psalm 110:1 always use the particle ἕως, further strengthening this view.

> For David is not ascended into the heavens: but **he saith himself**, The LORD said unto my Lord, Sit thou *on my right hand,* **until** (*ἕως*) I make thy foes thy footstool. *[notice David is said to speak these words "**himself**," further proving this is **not** an intra-dialogue between eternally divine 'persons'].* (Acts 2:34-35).
>
> But to which of the angels said he at any time, Sit *on my right hand,* **until** (*ἕως*) I make thine enemies thy footstool? (Hebrews 1:13).

Given the textual evidence—there is **no doubt** that Psalms 110:1 places a *time constraint* on the Messiah's session at '*the right hand*' through its use of the word "*until*." Yet, how is this reconciled with the Biblical truth regarding the Messiah's eternal priesthood?

> As he saith also in another place, Thou art a priest for ever after the order of Melchisedec (Hebrews 5:6).
>
> ...the forerunner is for us entered, even Jesus, made an high priest for ever after the order of Melchisedec (Hebrews 6:20).

---

[82] James Strong, עַד.

[83] Jouon, עַד.

[84] Carl Schultz, עַד, in (TWOT), electronic edition.

[85] Alfred Rahlfs, edt., Greek Septuagint, (Stuttgart, Germany: Deutsche Bibelgesellschaft, 2006) electronic edition with Septuagint Morphology Database, 2012.

[86] Danker, ἕως.

[87] Thayer, ἕως.

> For he testifieth, Thou art a <u>priest for ever</u> after the order of Melchisedec (Hebrews 7:17).
>
> ...but this with an oath by him that said unto him, the Lord sware and will not repent, Thou art a <u>priest for ever</u> after the order of Melchisedec (Hebrews 7:21).
>
> But this man, because he continueth ever, hath an <u>unchangeable priesthood</u> (Hebrews 7:24).

Scripture teaches the glorified man—Christ Jesus is a High Priest <u>forever</u> after the order of Melchizedek. While his priestly work includes *redemption and mediation*—Scripture **never** designates one as the High Priest by virtue of <u>*priestly works*</u> because this is **not** "*...a vocation <u>but an office</u>.*"[88] Thus, the *time limit* (*until*) placed on the Messiah's session at God's *'right hand'* is **not** addressing his eternal priesthood.

The glorified Messiah—Jesus Christ, eternally holds the <u>office</u> of High Priest—as <u>human</u> and <u>divine</u>—the <u>visible image of the invisible God</u>. Yet, the priestly works of <u>*redemption*</u> *and* <u>*mediation*</u> are linked to human salvation—which is within the <u>*sphere of time*</u>. Thus, while the '<u>*result*</u>' or '<u>*effect*</u>' of Jesus' priestly work is eternal, the salvific **experiences** associated with *redemption* and *mediation* culminates in the eschaton.

> But this man, because he continueth ever, hath an unchangeable priesthood. Wherefore he is able to **save them** to the uttermost that come **unto God** by him, seeing he ever liveth to make **intercession** for them (Hebrews 7:24-25).

The writer of Hebrews affirms the eternality of Jesus' priesthood and connects <u>*salvific-redemption*</u> and <u>*mediatory-intercession*</u> with the work of the glorified human Messiah (*i.e. 'this man'*). Yet, he uses the **present tense** in verse twenty-five when stressing the Messiah is able to <u>*save*</u> and <u>*ever lives*</u> to <u>make intercession</u> for those coming to God.[89] Thus, instead of referring to an *eternal work*—this passage teaches <u>*redemption*</u> and <u>*mediatory intercession*</u> are <u>present works</u> of the Messiah—which are *effected* or *realized* in the New Covenant salfivic experience (i.e. Acts 2:38).

---

[88] VanGemeren, כֹּהֵן. Emphasis mine.

[89] Robinson, *Hebrews 7:25*, <u>GNT</u> parsing interlinear and Morphological tagging standardized by Dr. Rex A. Koivisto, electronic edition.

Salvation is eternally durative; yet, the <u>experience of redemption</u> (*i.e., New Birth*) that provides the spiritual blessings of *justification, sanctification and Spirit baptism*—will culminate in believers *"final glorification in a life that never ends."*[90] This is why the church is commissioned to preach the Gospel until the close of this age.

> The promise of Christ to be with his Church, as then commissioned, to the end of the world, implies that its obligation to teach the nations is to continue until the final consummation.[91]

Believers of every epoch in human history will eternally enjoy the benefits of salvation. Yet, Scripture reveals the <u>opportunity</u> to **<u>experientially participate</u>** in these Soteriological blessings ceases at the close of this age—when time gives way into eternity. When this takes place—the <u>present</u> Messianic work of *redemption* and *mediatory-intercession* at God's *'right hand'* will be fully realized. Psalm 110:1 provides insight into this eschatological event, plainly revealing the Messiah remains at the right hand *"...until I make thine enemies thy footstool."*

There can be no debate that Psalm 110:1 teaches the subjugation of the Messiah's enemies will usher in a discernible <u>change</u>. This is especially clear in the Hebrew text, which unites the particle עַד (*until*) to the <u>*imperfect tense verb*</u> אָשִׁית (*I make*).[92] This is significant because:

> **with impf.**, of *future* time...in poetry, עַד is sometimes used to mark not an absolute close, but an epoch, or turning-point, in the future.[93]

The writer of Hebrews confirms the idea of inaugurating a 'new epoch' when he declares:

> But **this man**, after he had offered one sacrifice for sins for ever, sat down on the right hand of God; From henceforth **expecting till** his enemies be made his footstool (Hebrews 10:12-13).

---

[90] Berkhof, *Man in the Covenant of Grace*, <u>Summary of Christian Doctrine</u>.
[91] Charles Hodge, *The Calling of the Gentiles*, <u>Hodge's Systematic Theology</u>, electronic edition.
[92] Schenker, *Psalm 110:1*, <u>BHS</u>.
[93] Brown, Driver, Briggs, עַד. Emphasis mine.

This passage accents the permanency of the Messiah's redemptive work—specifically focusing on his sacrifice for sin—described as εἰς τὸ διηνεκές. The Greek word διηνεκές is defined as "*...always of time...for all time, without interruption;*"[94] thus, confirming that the Messiah's sin offering is a once *for all time* sacrifice.

In addition, the text teaches that, **subsequent** *to his sacrifice*, the Messiah sat down *'on the right hand of God.'* This statement clearly links redemption to the priestly work exercised at *the right hand*.

> The saving character of this historically unrepeatable fact is decisive and unending. What the High Priest Jesus completed on the human level is therefore the centre of all events, the **decisive midpoint of time**.[95]

Having previously referred to the ongoing priestly work of mediatory intercession (*i.e. 7:24-25*) the writer does not deal with this issue a second time in Heb. 10:12-13. Instead, he immediately transitions to the culmination of Psalm 110:1—signified by the use of τὸ λοιπόν (*'from henceforth'*) The word λοιπός is sometimes used adjectivally—referring to something that remains (*i.e. Rev. 8:13*).[96] Yet, in relation to time—τὸ λοιπόν is used adverbially signifying:[97]

> ...from now on, in the future, henceforth...as far as the rest is concerned, beyond that, in addition, finally...[98]

According to Hebrews 10:13—"*Finally, from now on,*" **after** the redemptive offering for sin and concurrent mediatory-intercession the writer describes the Messiah as ἐκδεχόμενος ἕως. The KJV renders this phrase *'expecting until'*—while other translations use "*waiting*" or "*waited.*"[99] Both meanings are encompassed in the Greek word ἐκδεχόμενος, which expresses the idea: "*..to continue to

---

[94] Danker, διηνεκής.

[95] Oscar Cullman, The Christology of the New Testament, (Grand Rapids, MI: Baker, 1954), 99. Emphasis mine.

[96] Louw & Nida, λοιπός.

[97] Rex A. Koivisto, *Morphological Tagging* in GNT, electronic Parsing tool Accordance Bible Software.

[98] Danker, λοιπός.

[99] The New International Version; The New Testament: Translated from the Syriac Peshito Version, (James Murdock, 1851).

*remain in a state <u>until an expected event</u>."*[100] The concept of *waiting until* is further emphasized by the particle ἕως (until) signifying:

> the temporal terminus ad quem, till, until...where something is spoken of which continued up to a certain time.[101]

Hebrews 7:24-25 affirms the eternality of Messiah's priesthood; yet, Hebrews 10:12-13 reveals a *temporal facet* to the redemptive-mediatory session at *'the right hand of God.'* Like Psalm 110:1-4, the writer of Hebrews teaches the glorified Messiah occupies the *'right hand'* position **until** all enemies are subjugated unto Him. This is significant—because it is an explicit declaration that there will be a <u>change</u> or <u>turning point</u> relative to the priestly session at the *right hand*—after all enemies are placed under His feet!

The Bible clearly teaches the Messiah is the eternal High Priest (*Psalm 110:4; Hebrews 5:6; 6:20; 7:17, 21, 24*). Therefore, the time constraint (**until**) placed on the Messiah's occupation at the *"right hand of God"* **cannot** refer to abolishing his eternal priestly <u>Office</u>. Rather, it speaks to the <u>present</u> work of <u>redemption</u> and <u>mediatory intercession</u>, which is a <u>corollary</u> of the Messiah's exaltation to *'the right hand of God'* (*i.e. Hebrews 7:24-25; 10:12-13*). In short, <u>redemption</u> and <u>mediation</u> are explicitly linked to <u>human salvific history</u>—which is foreordained to **eschatologically** culminate!

The New Testament teaches that Psalm 110:1-4 has been <u>*partially realized*</u> in the Messiah's glorification and exaltation. Therefore, it is impossible to properly interpret Jesus' placement at '*the right hand'* independent of the *<u>incarnation</u>* and *<u>glorification</u>* events. Further, the Hebrew, Greek and English texts of Psalm 110:1—shows that the Messiah's exaltation to the *"right hand of God" is temporal (until)* culminating with the subjugation of <u>all enemies</u>. This will result in an eschatological *'epoch'* or decisive *'turning point'* with respect to the Messiah's session at the right hand.

The decisive epoch following the fulfillment of Psalm 110:1 to *"...make thine enemies thy footstool"* is an eschatological event that marks the culmination of the *experiential process* of <u>redemption</u> and

---

[100] Louw & Nida, ἐκδέχομαι. Emphais mine.
[101] Thayer, ἕως.

<u>mediation</u>. These present salvific works are specifically linked to the High Priestly office and the Messianic '<u>right hand</u>' position. This helps explain why Jesus is **not** depicted at God's '*right hand*' in the Old Testament or in the Apocalypse of John (*i.e. Revelation 22:1-5*). In truth, when used of the Messiah, '<u>*right hand of God*</u>' is primarily a <u>soteriological</u> designator related to the *redemptive-mediatory* work of the glorified 'Christ.'

# IV

# The Eschatological Abdication of the 'Right Hand'

Information regarding the eschatological dimension of the Messiah's Priestly office and mediatory work is discovered in the Sixteenth chapter of John. This chapter forms a portion of Jesus' final discourse to His disciples prior to the crucifixion. Much of the content addresses the work of the Spirit of Christ subsequent to his resurrection and ascension. Yet, John 16:23-26 deserves special attention—for this passage addresses the *eschaton* and *the culmination* of Jesus' <u>mediatory work</u>.

John 16:23-26 does not cite Psalm 110:1-4 nor does it refer to the *'right hand of God.'* However, the text emphasizes Jesus' mediation, which is directly connected to His <u>glorification</u> and <u>exaltation</u> to the High Priestly office at the *'right hand of God'* (*i.e. Psalm 110:1-4; Hebrews 6:20; 7:21-25*). The use of *mediatory language* in these verses affirms a distinction between the <u>Father</u> and the <u>Son</u>. Yet, there is no indication this refers to *eternal hypostases;* rather, the distinction is clearly related to the incarnation—which is evident in Jesus' **revelatory disclosure** concerning His work of *mediation*.

Most commentators regard this section of John's Gospel as a reference to the coming Spirit poured out subsequent to Jesus' resurrection and ascension. This is substantiated in John 16:21-22 using the illustration of a woman whose travail and sorrow in labor is replaced with joy at the birth of her child. Though they did not fully understand—Jesus explains to his disciples they will have an similar experience with respect to his coming departure and return. He then states:

> And **in that day** ye shall ask me nothing. Verily, verily, I say unto you, Whatsoever ye shall ask the Father in my name, he will give it you. Hitherto have ye asked nothing in my name: ask, and ye shall receive, that your joy may be full (John 16:23-24).

Some believe *'that day'* is simply referring to the resurrection. While encompassing the resurrection—the context of John 16:23-26 includes Jesus' ministry following the <u>resurrection, glorification</u> and <u>ascension</u> to the mediatory *right hand*—and **looks forward** to the coming eschaton.

That **day,** in its full meaning cannot import *the forty days:* for,

> Acts 1:6, they did then *ask* the Lord *questions*—nor this present dispensation of the Spirit...but that great completion of the Christian's hope, when he shall be with his Lord...[102]
>
> ...we understand 'In that day' here in John 16:23; having both a narrower and wider meaning,...The Lord...intends this 'in that day' to include tint of all, the whole period of the dispensation of the Spirit...and then, pre-eminently, the end of this time, the *consummation of the fulness of the Spirit*...[103]

The idea '**that day**' refers to the <u>eschatological</u> day is strengthened by the twenty-fifth verse.

> <u>These things</u> have I spoken unto you in **proverbs**: but **the time cometh**, when I shall **no more** speak unto you **in proverbs**, but I shall shew you **plainly** of the Father. (John 16:25).

Jesus mention to "*these things*" refers to his ***mediatory statements*** recorded in verse twenty-three and twenty-four.

> ....ye shall <u>ask me</u> nothing...whatsoever ye shall <u>ask the Father</u> in <u>my name</u>, <u>he will give</u> it to you. Hitherto ye have asked nothing in my name, ask and ye shall receive...(John 16:23-24).

Sadly, many post-modern believers interpret this *subordinate mediatory language* literally. In fact, it is often used in an effort to 'prove' the concept of eternal distinctions in the Godhead. Yet, the twenty-fifth verse teaches the mediatory language "***These things***" (i.e., 'ask me nothing' 'ask the father...he will give it' 'ye have asked nothing in my name ask and ye shall receive') is actually proverbial language ('<u>proverbs</u>').

The word 'proverbs' is translated from the Greek παροιμίαις (*par-oi-mee-ah-is*) meaning:

> a brief communication containing truths designed for initiates, veiled saying, figure of speech, in which especially lofty ideas are concealed.[104]
>
> a saying out of the usual course or deviating from the usual manner of speaking...any dark saying which shadows forth some didactic truth especially a symbolic or figurative saying...[105]

---

[102] Henry Alford, <u>The New Testament for English Readers</u>, vol. 1. (Cambridge, England, 1863) 602.

[103] Arthur W. Pink, <u>Exposition of the Gospel of John</u>, Chapter 56, online edition <u>www.pbministries.org</u>.

[104] Danker, παροιμία.

[105] Thayer, παροιμία.

Jesus' use of *'proverbs'* does not mean the mediatory language is *'unreal'* or *'disingenuous.'* Yet, it emphasizes this is **enigmatic** or *'veiled speech'* **that requires an interpretation**; thus, it is not to be interpreted literally. Most importantly—in verse twenty-five, Jesus reveals he will **not** always use enigmatic speech in reference to the Father but he declares: ἔρχεται ὥρα *(the time [hour] comes)* ὅτε οὐκέτι ἐν παροιμίαις λαλήσω ὑμῖν *(when no longer in proverbs will I speak to you).*[106]

According to John 16:25, the 'hour' is marked by two concurrent events. First, Jesus promises to abolish the proverbial mediatory speech (*i.e. referring to the Father*). Second, he says παρρησίᾳ περὶ τοῦ πατρὸς ἀναγγελῶ ὑμῖν *(I will disclose to you plainly [openly] concerning [about] the Father).* It is significant that παροιμίαις *(pair-oi-mee-ah-is—**proverbs**)* is **intentionally juxtaposed** with παρρησίᾳ *(pair-hey-seeah—**plainly**).* This is especially true considering the former stresses the idea of *'veiled speech'*, while the latter refers to:

> ...speech that conceals nothing and passes over nothing, outspokenness, frankness, plainness.[107]
> This freedom of speech implies the truth of what is said, so that *parrhesia* means candor, straightforwardness...to speak candidly, proclaim the truth, and eschew evasions...[108]

John 16:25 looks forward to the time when Jesus no longer uses subordinate veiled language concerning the Father. Rather, he promises that *openly* or *plainly* ἀναγγελῶ ὑμῖν *(I will declare to you)* περὶ τοῦ πατρὸς *(concerning of the Father).* The word ἀναγγέλλω means *"to declare, announce, report, show or speak"*[109] or *"to provide information, with the possible implication of considerable detail."*[110]

Some may think Jesus' plain declaration of the Father occurred after His resurrection but prior to His ascension. Yet, there are two reasons this *open declaration concerning the Father* should be viewed

---

[106] ὥρα (hour) can denote a literal 24 hour period or simply the time or occasion of an event—as in this verse (*see Louw & Nida, ὥρα*).
[107] Danker, παρρησία.
[108] Spicq, παρρησία.
[109] Strong, ἀναγγέλλω.
[110] Louw & Nida, ἀναγγέλλω'.

as an <u>eschatological revelatory event</u>. First, Scripture reveals Jesus continued to use veiled mediatory language concerning the Father **after** his resurrection (*John 20:17; 20:21; Acts 1:4-7*). Second, Jesus provides an <u>explicit marker</u> or <u>designator</u> signaling the fulfillment of His promise to '**plainly**' reveal the Father in John 16:26.

> **At that day** ye shall ask in my name: and **I say not unto you, that I will pray the Father for you** (John 16:26).

The Greek text begins with the preposition Ἐν (in) coupled with the demonstrative pronoun ἐκείνῃ (that). This is followed by the word '<u>day</u>,' used with the definite article—τῇ ἡμέρᾳ (*lit. **the** day*). This is significant because the Greek article:

> ...is associated with gesture and aids in pointing out like an index finger. It is a pointer...The demonstrative may be used besides the article. Whenever the Greek article occurs, the object is certainly definite...The article is never meaningless in Greek.[111]

In Classical and Koine Greek (*i.e. New Testament*)—the article functioned "*...as a demonstrative pronoun;*"[112] thus, when used <u>with</u> a demonstrative pronoun (*i.e. ἐκείνῃ that*) it is "*...in a sense a double demonstrative.*"[113] This strongly indicates Ἐν ἐκείνῃ τῇ ἡμέρᾳ (*in **that, the** day*) refers to a <u>specific</u> time and event. Further evidence proving "**the day**" is used eschatologically is discovered in the words that follow wherein Jesus declares—ἐν τῷ ὀνόματί μου αἰτήσεσθε καὶ οὐ λέγω ὑμῖν ὅτι ἐγὼ ἐρωτήσω τὸν πατέρα περὶ ὑμῶν (*in the <u>name of me</u> you shall ask and <u>I will not say</u> that <u>I will ask [or pray] the Father</u> for [on account of] you*).

The import of '<u>the day</u>' in John 16:26 is not that disciples will *ask* (αἰτήσεσθε—*to ask, desire*)[114] <u>in my name</u>," Indeed, the Bible reveals the disciples used his name **prior** to the resurrection (*i.e., Mark 9:38-39; Luke 9:48-50; 10:1, 17*). Rather, the significance of '<u>the day</u>' is <u>when they ask in his name</u> Jesus will NO LONGER '*<u>pray the</u>*

---

[111] A. T. Robertson, *The Greek Article,* in <u>Grammar of the Greek New Testament in the Light of Historical Research</u>, electronic edition.

[112] Gerald L. Stevens, *The Definite Article,* in <u>New Testament Greek</u>, second edition, 1997, electronic format.

[113] Robertson, *The Greek Article.*

[114] Strongs, αἰτήσεσθε.

*Father'* for them. The word rendered 'pray' is ἐρωτήσω, meaning: *"to ask i.e. to request, entreat, beg, beseech."*¹¹⁵ This word is used in Jesus' priestly prayer (John 17); thus, it is clearly associated with the concept of *mediatory-intercession*.

> I pray (ἐρωτῶ) for them: I pray (ἐρωτῶ) not for the world...I pray (ἐρωτῶ) not that thou shouldest take them out of the world...Neither pray (ἐρωτῶ) I for these alone, but for them also which shall believe on me through their word (John 17:9, 15, 20).

John 16:25-26 teaches '**the day**' Jesus plainly reveals the Father also marks an end to His use of *proverbial-mediatory language in reference to the Father*. This is noteworthy since *'mediation'* is a priestly work of the High Priest—which is clearly a component of the Messiah's exaltation to the *'right hand of God' (Psalm 110:1-4)*. Moreover, there is strong evidence suggesting the *revelation of the Father* coincides with the fulfillment of Psalm 110:1-4. The Apostle Paul speaks to the eschatological realization of this prophecy and its relationship to the culmination of *mediatory 'Sonship'* in 1Corinthians 15:24-28.

Contextually, Paul's discussion concerning Psalm 110:1-4 follows his teaching on the resurrection of believers.

> Then cometh **the end**, when he shall have delivered up the kingdom to God, even **the Father**; when he shall have put down all rule and all authority and power (1Corinthians 15:24).

There is little doubt that Paul is referring to the coming eschaton though his use of εἶτα τὸ τέλος *(lit. then [next] the end)*. The word εἶτα (then) is an adverb that:

> pertains to being next in order of time...a transition word to mark an addition to something just stated, furthermore, then, next...introducing a new argument in a demonstration.¹¹⁶

According to the Apostle—the resurrection ushers in τὸ τέλος *(the end)* which denotes:

> ...the point aimed at a limit, i.e. (by implication) the conclusion of an act or state (termination literally, figuratively or

---

¹¹⁵ Thayer, ἐρωτάω. This is not the usual word for prayer. It is most often used in of inquiries.

¹¹⁶ Danker, εἶτα.

indefinitely), result (immediate, ultimate or prophetic)...[117]

Paul's use of the Greek article τὸ with τέλος emphasizes '<u>**the**</u> end' is a <u>specific period</u>. Contextually this is an eschatological event, for it is signified by the delivering up of the '<u>Kingdom to God</u>' <u>**after**</u> 'HE' has '*put down*, καταργήσῃ (*"cause something to lose its power...cause something to come to an end...abolish, wipe out, set aside"*)[118] all rule, power and all authority.

Perhaps of greater significance—the Apostle links '**the end**' with the final realization of Psalm 110:1-4 saying,

> For <u>he must reign,</u> <u>**till**</u> <u>he hath put all enemies under his feet</u> (1Corinthians 15:25).

Paul's statement is a citation of the final portion of Psalm 110:1. Yet, unlike the Septuagint rendering or the quotation of this text in the book of Hebrews (*i.e., Heb. 10:12-13*) Paul does not use ἕως to express the idea of '<u>until</u>.'[119]

Instead of ἕως the Apostle intentionally uses the more <u>forceful</u> phrase ἄχρι οὗ ἄν to stress the *time constraint* (***until***) placed on the Messiah's session at the '*right hand.*' The word ἄχρι (*until*) is used with a genitive; thus, it functions as a preposition denoting "*until, as far as;*"[120] "*the continuous extent of time up to a point—until.*"[121]

The force of ἄχρι (*until*) is increased by the use of the particle ἄν. Though incapable of being translated by one English word,[122] the particle expresses the idea of certainty when particular conditions are met.[123] Indeed, ἄν:

> ...denotes that the action of the verb is dependent on some

---

[117] Τέλος, in <u>Key Dictionary of the Greek New Testament</u>, electronic edition, Oak Tree Software Inc.

[118] Danker, καταργέω.

[119] Alfred Rahlfs, edt., *Psalm 110:1,* <u>The Greek Septuagint</u>, electronic edition. (see Robinson, Hebrews 10:12-13 GNT).

[120] Thomas, Robert edt., ἄχρι, <u>NAS Greek Dictionary</u>, electronic edition.

[121] Louw & Nida, ἄχρι.

[122] Lust, J., E. Eynikel, ἄν, <u>A Greek - English Lexicon of the Septuagint, Second Edition</u> (LEH-2) electronic format.

[123] Louw & Nida, ἄν.

circumstance or condition...especially after relatives...[124]

a particle indicating that something can or could occur on certain conditions, or by the combination of certain fortuitous causes.[125]

1Cor. 15:25 reveals the primary **condition** governing the **certain** fulfillment of the Messiah's session at the *right hand* is realized when θῇ (*he has placed*) πάντας τοὺς ἐχθροὺς (*all the enemies*) ὑπὸ Τοὺς πόδασ αὐτοῦ (*under the feet of him*).[126] In other words, through his use of the powerful contingency phrase ἄχρι οὗ ἂν the Apostle Paul confirms the Messiah will remain at the *"right hand"* **until the condition of placing all enemies under His feet is realized!** Further evidence this occurs in the eschaton—is found in the next verse.

The last enemy that shall be destroyed is death (1Corinthians 15:26).

The Greek word "last" is ἔσχατος (eschatos)—a noun that means *"being last in a series of objects or events—last, final, finally."*[127] While this word does not always refer to the eternal eschaton—there is little doubt this is the intended meaning of this verse. Indeed, the entire context reveals this is the period when the kingdom of the redeemed are in God's presence and the enemy—θάνατος (death) is vanquished— Praise God! Most importantly, this eschatological event is the culmination of Psalm 110:1-4—bringing the *redemptive work of the right hand mediatory position*—to a glorious conclusion.

The Apostle provides greater insight into this event by revealing what transpires **after** all enemies have been subjugated and under the Messiah's feet.

For **he hath put all things under his feet**. But when he saith, all things are put under him, it is manifest that he is excepted, which did put all things under him (1Corinthians 15:27).

The above verse reiterates the promise of Psalm 110:1 but includes δῆλον ὅτι ἐκτὸς τοῦ ὑποτάξαντος αὐτῷ τὰ πάντα (lit. *[it is] certain [evident or manifest] that the one who subjected all to him is an*

---

[124] Danker, ἄν.

[125] Thayer, ἄν.

[126] Robinson, GNT, author's literal translation.

[127] Louw & Nida, ἔσχατος.

*exception).*

The above statement is a reminder that the <u>time constraint</u> (*until*) of Psalm 110:1 is **not applicable** to the one responsible for placing all things under the feet of the <u>glorified human Messiah</u>. This does not indicate there are eternal hypostases in God—rather, it affirms Psalm 110:1-4 **must** be viewed in the **context of the incarnation**. Indeed, it is the one true God that places all enemies under the feet of the glorified man, Christ Jesus—in whom the fulness of the Godhead dwells. This is especially clear in the next verse.

> And when all things shall be subdued unto him, then shall **the Son also himself be subject unto him** that put all things under him, **that God may be all in all** (1Corinthians 15:28).

The Greek text says: "Ὅταν δὲ ὑποταγῇ αὐτῷ τὰ πάντα *(but when all [things] have been subjected to him)* τότε καὶ αὐτός ὁ υἱὸς ὑποταγήσεται *(lit. then even [also] himself, the son will be subjected)*.[128] It is interesting that ὑποταγήσεται *(subjected)* is used in reference to the 'Son' since ὑποτάσσω means "*to cause to be in a submissive relationship, to subject, to subordinate.*"[129]

> to make subordinate, submit, append, attach..."submission," which should not be confused with obedience, is a major virtue in the Christian pastoral writings, expressing the relations of subordination in the cosmic and religious order.[130]

The above writer (Spicq) is obviously concerned with making a distinction between <u>submission</u> and <u>obedience</u> in his definition of the word ὑποτάσσω. Perhaps this is because it is used of "the Son" in 1Cor. 15:28. Clearly—this is problematic **if** "**the Son**" is viewed as *the second hypostasis in the Godhead*. While Spicq correctly notes that '*submission*' is **not** identical to '*obedience*,' he is well aware of the fact that the New Testament uses ὑποτάσσω and its derivatives (*i.e.*, ὑποταγήσετ) to stress <u>obedience</u>; in fact, he admits:

> The literal meaning of ὑποτάσσομαι is "<u>to order oneself under</u>" a leader..To submit is to <u>accept directives</u> that are given, to honor conditions that are imposed, to <u>please one's superior</u>

---

[128] Robinson, *1Corinthians 15:28*, <u>GNT</u>. Author's translation with Greek-English interlinear.

[129] Danker, ὑποτάσσω.

[130] Spicq, ὑποτάσσω.

(Titus 2:9) or honor him by the homage <u>that is obedience</u> (cf. Eph 6:1)...[131]

It is true ὑποτάσσω does not imply inferiority and there are times when the word stresses self-submission, "*to subject oneself, to obey; to submit to one's control...*"[132] Yet, the idea of 'self-submission' is not germane to this word. In fact, the Greek language primarily uses '**voice**' to convey "*...the relationship of the verb's action to the verb's subject.*"[133] This is significant because—unlike the two voice (active/passive) system of English—the Greek language possesses a third <u>participatory</u> voice referred to as the '*middle voice*' wherein:

> the verb's subject is *reflecting* the verb's action, in two ways... the *direct* middle...the verb's subject is reflecting directly the action of the verb onto itself...the *indirect* middle, in which the subject is acting with self-interest in the action.[134]

In short, if the intent of ὑποτάσσω is to convey "*self-subjection,*" one reasonably expects the middle voice to be used, as Paul does in Eph. 5:24 (*ὑποτάσσεται*). Yet, when speaking of the subjection of '*the Son*' in 1Cor. 15:28—the Apostle Paul does **not** use the <u>middle</u> voice. Rather, he intentionally uses the <u>passive</u> voice to describe the subjection of "*all things,*" **as well as** the subjection of *the Son.*[135] This is important because when the passive voice is used:

> The subject is represented as the recipient of the action. He is acted upon.[136]

> The verb's subject passively *receives* the verb's action ("I am being poured out," Phil 2:17).[137]

> The passive voice indicates that the subject is the one being acted upon. For example, in the sentence "*He was stopped,*" the verb "*was stopped*" is in the passive voice, indicating that the subject was the one who received the action.[138]

---

[131] Ibid.

[132] Thayer, ὑποτάσσω.

[133] Stevens, *Greek Verb Components—Voice.*

[134] Ibid.

[135] Robinson, *1Corinthians 15:28,* <u>GNT</u> with English Interlinear and Parsing tool.

[136] Robertson, *Passive Voice.*

[137] Stevens, *Greek Verb Components—Voice.*

[138] Stephen Marler, edt., <u>Parsing Guide to the Greek text of the KJV</u> electronic edition.

In other words, 1Cor. 15 28 does not depict a *'self-subjection'* of 'the Son, but states: καὶ (*and/even*) αὐτός ὁ υἱὸς (*himself the son*) ὑποταγήσεται (*he shall be subjected*)![139] Those embracing 'Eternal Sonship' or believe *the Son* is a *hypostasis of God*, face a significant dilemma in this verse. Indeed, this would mean the *'co-equal,' 'co-eternal,' 'consubstantial'* hypostasis of '**the Son**' is *passively subjected* to *another hypostasis* of God. This is nonsensical since Paul plainly states **the reason** for the Son's subjection is—ἵνα (*in order that*) ᾖ (*he may be*) ὁ θεὸς (*the God*) τὰ πάντα ἐν πᾶσιν (*the all in all*).

The Greek conjunction ἵνα denotes "*purpose, aim, or goal, in order that, that, final sense*"[140] and in 1Cor. 15:28 it is used with the present subjunctive verb ᾖ (*may exist or be*). The subjunctive mood denotes contingency or anticipation and when expressing *purpose* or *result* it is normally used in a ἵνα clause.[141] In fact, at the time of the New Testament—the ἵνα clause was "*...almost the exclusive means of expressing purpose.*"[142] Thus, using ἵνα with the subjunctive (ᾖ) forms a final clause that expresses the *purpose* of the stated action.[143]

In short, 1Cor. 15:28 reveals the purpose and result of the Son's subjection is that ὁ θεὸς (*the God)* may be all in all. This argues **against** any interpretation suggesting 'the Son' is a hypostasis of God and-or that the *right hand* is a literal physical location! In fact, such a view would mean "the Son" is **not** '**The God**' or that there are two beings in spatial relationship—only one of whom is '**the God.**' Unfortunately, this leads to the conclusion that:

> ...the last of the eschatological events prior to the eternal state will be the subjection of the Son to the Father and that this will

---

[139] Ibid., *1Corinthians 15:28*. Interestingly, Robertson suggests the use of the passive in this verse has the "force" of a middle; however, this is a theological interpretation rather than examining the normative use of the passive in the New Testament—especially in Paul's epistles.

[140] Danker, ἵνα.

[141] Stevens, *The Subjunctive Mood*

[142] Robertson, ἵνα.

[143] Ernest De Witt Burton, *Pure Final Clauses*, in Syntax of the Moods and Tenses in New Testament Greek, electronic edition.

be the condition forever thereafter.[144]

In reality—it is impossible to properly interpret this text without grasping the *dual identity* of 'the Son' as simultaneously '*the God*' and a *genuine human*. Indeed, Scripture **never** uses the designator 'Son' with reference to a singular *hypostasis* of God. Moreover, used of Jesus—"*the Son*" **always** denotes the visible localization or incarnation of '*the God*' in the person and name of Jesus.

> Who is the image of the invisible God (ὅς ἐστιν εἰκὼν τοῦ θεοῦ τοῦ ἀοράτου—*who is the icon of THE God the one who is invisible*) Colossians 1:15.
>
> For in him dwelleth all the fulness of the Godhead bodily. (ὅτι ἐν αὐτῷ κατοικεῖ πᾶν τὸ πλήρωμα τῆς θεότητος σωματικῶς— That in him he dwells all the fullness, sum total of THE Godhead in bodily form) Colossians 2:9.
>
> For this is good and acceptable in the sight of God our Saviour (τοῦτο γὰρ καλὸν καὶ Ἀπόδεκτον ἐνώπιον τοῦ σωτῆρος ἡμῶν θεοῦ—for this is good and pleasing before in the sight of THE God savior of ours) 1Timothy 2:3.
>
> Looking for that blessed hope, and the glorious appearing of the great God and our Saviour Jesus Christ (τοῦ μεγάλου θεου καὶ σωτῆρος ἡμῶν Ιησοῦ χριστοῦ—*THE great God and [even] savior of us Jesus Christ*) Titus 2:13.

The above citations represent only a portion of New Testament verses that identify '*the Son*' as the visible personification of '*the God*.' Yet, it is important to point out that each of these verses are a part of the Pauline corpus! This forces one to ask: "*How can Paul believe* '**the Son**' *is the visible localization of* '**the God**' (Col. 1:15; Titus 2:13) *and also teach* 'the Son' *is* subjected *in order that* '**The God**' *may be all in all*" (1Cor 15:27-28)? This is answered when one realizes these passages highlight different aspects of '*the Son's*' identity. For example, Col. 1:15; 2:9 emphasizes the Son's **Divinity** as '**the God**' while 1Cor. 15: 27-28 accentuates his **genuine humanity**.

Regardless of his *specific emphasis* Paul affirms the simultaneous **dual identity** of 'the Son' as a genuine 'human' **AND** the visible localization of 'the God.' Thus, a proper interpretation of 1Cor. 15: 25-28 is **only** achieved by examining the passage in light of the

---

[144] John V. Dahms, *The Subordination of the Son*, in Journal of the Evangelical Theological Society 37/3 (Louisville, KY: Evangelical Theological Society, September, 1994), 352.

truth that the Deity resident **in** '*the Son*' is '**The God**'! In fact, this is essential for reconciling Paul's seemingly contradictory statements concerning "*the Son*" and avoiding the errors of *ditheism* and-or *arianism*.

Of course, this leads to a critical question that one must consider, namely:

> How can '**the Son**' be subject to '**the God**' if the Deity *residing in* '**the Son**' is '**the God**'—who, according to Paul, is '*excepted*' *from subjection* (1Cor. 15:27)?

The answer to this is discovered only by recognizing the 1Cor. 15: 25-28 is a graphic portrayal of the culmination of Psalm 110:1 in the eschaton '*the end*.' It is **'the day'** when the *redemptive-mediatory* work at the '*right hand*' is completed because the salvific ***purpose*** for Yahweh's assumption of humanity is finally realized.

The Bible reveals "*the Son*" was *begotten* for the express purpose of human redemption and mediation. In other words, God **never needed** a Son—humanity did. Thus, for our sake (Isa. 9:6) Yahweh was visibly manifest in the person and name of Jesus for human salvation. Unlike the theophanies of the Old Testament—Yahweh fully and permanently incorporated humanity into His identity in and through His incarnation in "the Son." Yet, the salvific *work* of 'the Son' (i.e. *redemption and mediation*) is a temporal function of the '*right hand*' position—culminating in the eternal eschaton.

There is no question the *effects* of redemption and mediation are eternal; yet, the salvation experiences associated with these works (*i.e., justification, sanctification, Spirit Baptism*) reach an ***experiential conclusion*** when the redeemed are in the presence of the Lord and **all enemies**, *including death*, have been placed under the feet of the glorified Messiah. In other words, when Paul speaks of the '*Son's*' subjection in 1Cor. 15:28—he is not referring to an '*eternal person of God.*' Rather, his message "...*is soteriological and concentrates on the function of the Messianic agent (Christ).*"[145] Indeed, this passage refers to the climax of '*the Son's*' mediatory work **at** the *right hand!*

---

[145] Scott Lewis, "*So that God may be All in All,*" in Liber Annuus, XL IX (Jerusalem, Israel: Studium Biblicum Franciscanum, 1999), 209.

In truth, 1Cor. 15:24-26 is **not** an <u>ontological statement</u> regarding the composition of God's nature, but an <u>eschatological-soteriological</u> message concerning the culmination of human redemption. In fact, there is simply no way the subjection of '<u>The Son</u>' to '<u>The God</u>' can refer to the *person of Jesus* because the *Deity resident IN Jesus is the* **one God and Father**–that Paul says is ἐκτὸς (*outside, apart from, except*)[146] or **exempt** from **subjection!**

> Believest thou not that I am in the Father, and the **Father in me**? The words that I speak unto you I speak not of myself: but the **Father that dwelleth in me**, he doeth the works (John 14:10).
> For **in him dwelleth** all the fulness of the Godhead bodily (Colossians 2:9).

In John 14:10 Jesus clearly states the Deity **<u>residing in him</u>** is the **Father**! The Greek text is explicit:...ὁ δὲ πατὴρ (*but the Father*) ὁ ἐν ἐμοὶ μένων (*who in me is dwelling*). The preposition ἐν "*...denotes being or remaining within with the...idea of rest and continuance.*"[147] It is used here with the present active participle μένων, meaning:

> remain, stay...of a location stay, often in the special sense live, dwell, lodge.[148]
> A primary verb; to stay (in a given place, state, relation...abide, continue, dwell...)[149]

According to Jesus—the only Deity that is localized or resident **within Him** is the one God and Father! In Col. 2:9—Paul corroborates this truth saying: ὅτι ἐν αὐτῷ (*that in him*) κατοικεῖ (*continues to reside*) πᾶν τὸ Πλήρωμα τῆς θεότητος (*all the fulness of THE Deity*) σωματικῶς (*in bodily form*). Like John 14:10—the Apostle uses the preposition ἐν to describe the *"indwelling."*

> ...the idea of 'within,' whether of rest or of motion depending on the context...The preposition merely states that the location is within the bounds marked by the word with which it occurs. It does not mean 'near,' but 'in,' that is 'inside.'[150]

---

[146] Louw & Nida, ἐκτός.

[147] E. W. Bullinger, *"Notes and Appendixes"* in <u>The Companion Bible</u>, (Grand Rapids, MI: Kregel, 1999).

[148] Danker, μένω.

[149] Strong, μένω.

[150] A. T. Robertson, *Proper Prepositions in the N.T.*

The greatest difference between the two verses is that Col. 2:9 does not use a form of μένω to describe God's residency. Rather, Paul couples the preposition ἐν with the word κατοικεῖ, meaning: *"to live or dwell in a place in an established or settled manner."*[151] This is important considering Col. 2:9 is written after the resurrection and glorification of the Messiah! In short, the Apostle is not merely asserting God **was** fully resident *in 'the Son'* but purposely uses κατοικεῖ to stress the **permanency** of God's incarnation!

Colossians 2:9 emphatically declares the one true God *presently* and *permanently* resides in **him**—σωματικῶς, *"bodily, corporeally,"*[152]

> ...a physical body...in physical form. It is also possible to interpret σωματικῶς...pertaining to being real (in the sense of material) in contrast with being symbolic...[153]

This is significant because it demonstrates that the *subjection* of '*the Son*' does not refer to the *Divinity* or *humanity* of Jesus—because the Deity who is "*excepted*" from subjection—permanently resides in the glorified person and name of JESUS.

1Corinthians 15:24-28 is an eschatological glimpse at the closing of human salvation history and the culmination of the Messiah's *soteriological redemptive mediatory work*. In fact, neither Oneness nor Trinitarians interpret the subjection of the Son as referring to the person of Jesus. Rather, both understand 1Cor. 15:28 *functionally*, believing it is a reference to the completion the Son's Priestly session at *the right hand* in fulfillment of Psalm 110.

In truth, Trinitarian and Oneness scholars reject the notion that 1Cor. 15:28 teaches the person of the Son is "*...absorbed in God when the redemptive action has reached its goal.*"[154] Instead it is believed:

> ...the language of the subordination of the Son to the Father is functional, referring to his 'work' of redemption, not ontological, referring to his being as such. The unity of God lies behind all such language.[155]

---

[151] Louw & Nida, κατοικέω. Emphasis mine.

[152] Thayer, σωματικῶς.

[153] Louw & Nida, σωματικῶς.

[154] Cullman, 305.

[155] Gordon D. Fee, The First Epistle to the Corinthians, in The New International Commentary on the New Testament, (Grand Rapids, MI:

> It is best...to understand it of the Son's giving up...his mediatorial kingdom...when I say he will resign or lay aside his office as mediator, my meaning is...he will cease to administer that office as under God, in the manner he does now.[156]

This means the fulfillment of *the Son's* salvific mediation *at God's 'right hand'* is not an absolute termination—but a turning point in the functional role exercised by the glorified human Messiah.

> The interpretation which affirms that the Son shall then be subject to the Father in the sense of laying down his delegated authority, and ceasing to exercise his mediatorial reign, has been the common interpretation of all times.[157]

The culmination of **the Son's** *redemptive-mediatory* work represents the fulfillment of Jesus' two-fold promise to cease praying *"...the Father for you"* and revealing *"...plainly of the Father"* (John 16:25-26). The Apostle makes this clear by explaining that the *purpose or result* of the Son's subjection is *"...that **the** God may be **the all** in all."*

The above rendering amplifies the Greek Text's use of the article "The" before God (*The God*). Interestingly, in the phrase "all in all" the article is employed before the first occurrence of 'all' but not the latter—"τὰ πάντα **(the all)** ἐν πᾶσιν" (*in all)*. When used with the article—πᾶς (all) carries the idea of *entire, all or whole*; whereas, *without* the article, it denotes *"...each, every, all...full absolute, greatest."*[158] Thus, the eschatological subjection of *'The Son'* reveals God is the source of human redemption to include every salvific work exercised **in** and **through** 'The Son'!

The revelatory "day" of 'the end' described in Paul's letter to the Corinthians is also referenced in his Epistle to Timothy.

> That thou keep this commandment without spot, unrebukeable, until the appearing of **our Lord Jesus Christ**: Which **in his times** he shall shew, who is the blessed and **only** Potentate, the King of kings, and Lord of lords; Who **only** hath immortality, dwelling in the light which no man can approach unto; whom no man hath seen, nor can see: to whom be

---

Eerdmans, 1997), 760.

[156] John Gill, *1Corinthians 15:28*, in Gill's Exposition of the Entire Bible, online resource at www.bible.cc.

[157] Albert Barnes, *1Corinthians 15:28*, Barnes Notes on the Bible, online edition, www.bible.cc.

[158] Danker, πᾶς.

honour and power everlasting. Amen (1Timothy 6:14-16).

Contextually—the Apostle Paul refers to something that happens *after* the eschatological *appearing of the Lord*. It is a revelatory event that takes place καιροῖς ἰδίοις *(in his own times)*. Interestingly, instead of the pronoun αυτος *(him)* Paul uses the adjective ἰδίοις, expressing something private—*"one's own affairs, property, etc."*[159]

In 1 Timothy 6:15-16 the private or particular ἰδίοις is said to be the καιροῖς (times) belonging to Jesus Christ—'<u>The Son</u>.' Καιροῖς refers to a *"point of time or period of time...with the implication of being especially fit for something..."*[160] The word is frequently used with reference to eschatological events that focus on:

> ...the time from the return of Christ on, the times of the consummated divine kingdom...as often in Greek writings, and like the Latin *tempus*, **kairos;** is equivalent to *what time brings, the state of the times, the things and events of time.*[161]

At the specific point of time 'belonging' to the Lord—the Apostle declares the Lord—δείξει *(he will show)* which is a promise:

> to exhibit something that can be apprehended by one or more of the senses, point out, show, make known...to prove or make clear by evidence or reasoning, explain, prove.[162]
>
> To make known the character or significance of something by visual, auditory, gestural or linguistic means...to explain the meaning or significance of something by demonstration.[163]

The text continues by explaining the Lord will show or make known the identity of ὁ μακάριος καὶ μόνος δυνάστης *"the blessed and <u>only</u> ruler."* The word '**only**' (μόνος) is used as an adjective in this verse and *"...pertains to being the only entity in a class, only, alone adj. With a focus on being the only one."*[164] Paul couples this word with several descriptive nouns *(i.e., ruler or sovereign, King of kings and Lord of lords)* and culminates by emphasizing Jesus will reveal the *only one* who is immortal, invisible and omnipotent!

---

[159] Spicq, ἴδιος.
[160] Danker, καιρός.
[161] Thayer, καιρός.
[162] Danker, δείκνυμι.
[163] Louw & Nida, δείκνυμι.
[164] Danker, μόνος.

In other words, the Apostle Paul provides an additional witness that '*The Son*' reveals the identity of the **only true God** in a manner *plainly or openly apprehended!* Thus, 1 Timothy 6:14-16 corroborates Jesus' promise to *plainly reveal the Father at that day* (John 16:25-26) and gives further insight regarding the culmination of the Son's redemptive-mediatory work at God's right hand when the process of human redemption is complete (1Cor. 15:24-28).

# V

# From the Right Hand To The Center of the Throne

The plain revelation of the Father and *relative termination* of the redemptive-mediatory work of the *right hand place* is fully realized in the coming eschaton. Several verses in the Apocalypse of John speak to this truth—providing clarity concerning the fulfillment of Psalm 110:1 and the subsequent *"state"* or *"position"* occupied by Jesus throughout eternity.

> And **he that sat upon the throne** said, Behold I make all things new. And he said unto me, Write: for these words are true and faithful. And he said unto me, **It is done**. **I am Alpha and Omega**, the beginning and the end. I will give unto him that is athirst of the fountain of the water of life freely. He that overcometh shall inherit all things; **and I will be his God**, and he **shall be my son** (Revelation 21:5-7).

The above passage gives pertinent information concerning the eschatological position of Jesus. Yet, it is often *overlooked* because most *'red letter'* editions omit the red in this quote from the *"Alpha and Omega."* This is strange considering this title is used *three other times* in the book of Revelation—**always** with reference to Jesus and **always** typeset in *'red'* in these same editions!

> Behold, **he cometh with clouds**; and every eye shall see him, and they also which pierced him: and all kindreds of the earth shall wail because of him. Even so, Amen. **I am Alpha and Omega**, the beginning and the ending, saith the Lord, which is, and which was, and which is to come, the Almighty (Revelation 1:7-8).
>
> Saying, **I am Alpha and Omega**, the first and the last...And being turned, I saw seven golden candlesticks; And in the midst of the seven candlesticks one like unto **the Son of man**... (Revelation 1:11-13).
>
> And, behold, **I come quickly**; and my reward is with me, to give every man according as his work shall be. **I am Alpha and Omega**, the beginning and the end, the first and the last (Revelation 22:12-13).

Scripture plainly teaches there is *ONE* Alpha and Omega, *ONE* first and last, *ONE* Almighty and *ONE* which was, which is and is to come. Indeed, an honest reading of Scripture explicitly shows the **Alpha and Omega** of Revelation 21:6 is ***the same one*** referred to in Revelation 1:7-8, 11-13 and 22:12-13! In fact, this title is consistently used in the book of Revelation to identify the one who is simultaneously human and Divine—the glorified Messiah,

Jesus Christ! Thus, there is simply **no** grammatical basis to suggest the "*Alpha and Omega*" in Revelation 21:6 refers to someone other than the incarnate one—the Lord Jesus Christ!

If there are no linguistic grounds for interpreting the <u>Alpha and Omega</u> in Revelation 21:6 as *something other than* a Christological designation—why do most '*red letter*' editions omit the red? The answer is simply that most editorial committees hold a *theological view* that is contrary to the message of this verse and sadly, have allowed their *theological presupposition* to influence their treatment of this verse. This is especially evident when examining the **<u>contextual message</u>** of Revelation 21:1-7.

> And I saw a new heaven and a new earth...And I heard a great voice out of heaven saying, Behold, the tabernacle of God is with men, and he will dwell with them, and they shall be his people, and God himself shall be with them, and be their God (Revelation 21:1-3).

The twenty-first chapter of Revelation begins by providing a glimpse into the culmination of this age and the dawning of the new age. It is the day of a *'new heaven'* and *'new earth'* **and** marks the time when: ἡ **σκηνὴ** (*the tent-tabernacle*) τοῦ θεοῦ (*of **the** God*) μετὰ τῶν ἀνθρώπων (*[is] with humanity*) καὶ σκηνώσει μετ αὐτῶν (*and <u>He will tabernacle</u> with them*). John's reference to the *tabernacle of God* is significant—as the word σκηνὴ is deeply embedded in Hebraic thought and rich in symbolism; in fact the noun signifies:

> a portable dwelling of cloth and/or skins, held up by poles and fastened by cords or stakes...One should avoid terms which would imply a military tent or a temporary shelter used only on vacations or holidays. In OT times such tents were permanent dwellings of nomadic groups.[165]

In the Old Testament the "*tabernacle*" or "*tent of meeting*" was the portable structure where God <u>placed his name</u> and was visibly manifest in the glory cloud. Interestingly, the word σκηνὴ is used to describe the tabernacle in the Septuagint,[166] which is the same word used in Revelation 21:3 to describe the 'structure' encasing God's presence in eternity. Moreover, John declares: καὶ **σκηνώσει**

---

[165] Louw & Nida, σκηνὴ.
[166] Rahlfs., edt., <u>The Greek Septuagint</u>.

μετ αὐτῶν (and **he will reside** with them) καὶ αὐτοὶ λαὸς αὐτοῦ ἔσονται (and they will be His people) καὶ αὐτός ὁ θεὸς ἔσται μετ αὐτῶν (and he **the God** with them will be).

According to the text—**The God σκηνώσει** (*he dwells or resides*) *in* and *through* His visible tabernacle in the eschaton. The word '*he dwells*' (σκηνώσει) is a 3rd person singular verb meaning *"live, settle, take up residence."*[167] It is the verbal form of σκηνὴ (*tabernacle*); thus, literally denotes '*pitching*' a tent, "*to fix one's tabernacle...abide (or live) in a tabernacle (or tent)...*"[168] Does John's use of σκηνὴ and σκηνώσει suggest that God's presence will be encased in a visible structure in eternity? The answer to this is both YES *and* NO!

John's use of '*tabernacle*' in Revelation 21:1-3 does **not** refer to a physical building—like the Old Testament structure. Rather, his use of σκηνὴ and σκηνώσει coincides with the way he employs the verb σκηνόω in His gospel—*to graphically portray God's incarnation in the person and name of Jesus.*

> And the Word was made flesh, and **dwelt** among us, (and we beheld his glory, the glory as of the only begotten of the Father,) full of grace and truth (John 1:14).

The word *dwelt* (ἐσκήνωσεν *He dwelt*) is the *aorist tense 3rd person singular* form of σκηνόω.[169] John intentionally uses this terminology to depict how **the God** (John 1:1) *pitched His tent* **in** and **through** the incarnation! In short, God's '*tabernacle*' *of* and *in* flesh refers to Yahweh's visible localization in the person and name of Jesus, the human Messiah born in Bethlehem. Understood in this manner, the 'tabernacle' of Revelation 21:3 affirms the permanence and eternality of the incarnation—emphasizing God is visibly manifest and apprehended **in** and **through** the glorified man, Jesus Christ throughout eternity.

Further evidence showing the *tabernacle* of Revelation 21:3 refers to the glorified Messiah is revealed in the next four verses, which describe the events that occur in conjunction with the visible

---

[167] Danker, σκηνόω. Electronic parsing by Accordance Bible.
[168] Thayer, σκηνόω.
[169] Rex A. Koivisto, *'Morphological Tagging,'* GNT, electronic edition.

manifestation of *the tabernacle of God.*

> And God shall wipe away all tears from their eyes; and there shall be **no more death**, neither sorrow, nor crying, neither shall there be any more pain: for **the former things are passed away** (Revelation 21:4).

According to John—the revelation of God's tabernacle coincides with the *'passing away'* of the former things. The word used here is ἀπῆλθον, *"to go out of existence, cease to exist, to pass away"*[170]

John lists several things—*presently a part of the human condition,* that <u>cease</u> with the revelation of the tabernacle of God (*i.e. sorrow, tears, pain*). Yet, perhaps the most significant is his reference to the **abolishment of death**! Indeed, this indicates the manifestation of God's tabernacle is ***concurrent*** with the eschatological events that are referred to in 1Corinthians 15:24-28. In fact, Revelation 21:3-7 provides additional details regarding the "<u>state</u>" or "<u>position</u>" Jesus occupies **after** the culmination of the *redemptive-mediatory work* of Psalm 110:1 at the *'right hand of God.'*

Revelation 21:3-7 is the ***eschatological realization*** of 1Cor. 15:24-28; 1Tim. 6:13-16 and the fulfillment of Jesus's promise to *plainly reveal* the Father (Jhn. 16:23-26). This becomes especially evident in the continued description of this wonderful scene.

> And **he** that sat upon **the throne** said, Behold, **I** make all things new. And **he** said unto me, Write: for these words are true and faithful. And **he** said unto me, It is done. **I am Alpha and Omega**, the beginning and the end. **I** will give unto him that is athirst of the fountain of the water of life freely (Revelation 21:5-6).

The Greek text begins: καὶ εἶπεν *(and He said)* ὁ καθήμενος *(the one sitting)* ἐπὶ τῷ θρόνῳ *(upon the throne).*[171] This is a foundational statement for several reasons—including the fact it reiterates there is ***one throne*** under consideration.[172]

It is also significant that only ***one personage*** visibly <u>occupies</u> the **one throne**. This is confirmed through John's use of the singular

---

[170] Louw & Nida, ἀπέρχομαι.

[171] Robinson, *Revelation 21:5,* <u>GNT</u>, with English Interlinear.

[172] Rex A. Koivisto, *'Morphological Tagging,'* <u>GNT</u>, Θρόνῳ is a singular noun used in the Dative case in this verse.

participle ὁ καθήμενος, ('*the one sitting*') coupled with the third person singular verb λέγει (*he said*).[173] Most importantly—verse six identifies the one sitting on the throne as the **Alpha and Omega**, which is expressly revealed as the glorified Messiah—Jesus. Thus, Rev. 21:3-7 clearly teaches that—*subsequent to the culmination of Psalm 110:1*—Jesus is *no longer* depicted as *'standing'* or *'sitting'* on *'God's right hand.'* Rather, HE is the **one** seated on the throne!

As hitherto stated, the Alpha and Omega is a Christological title used exclusively in reference to the glorified Messiah, Jesus Christ (*i.e., Rev. 1:8, 11; 22:13*). This is essential to grasp because **HE** is the one who speaks in Revelation 21:6—and **HE** is the one who gives the twofold promise recorded in verse seven.

> He that overcometh shall inherit all things; and **I will be his God**, and **he shall be my son** (Revelation 21:7).

The text begins: Ὁ (THE) νικῶν (*nikon: one who prevails, conquers, overcomes*)[174] κληρονομήσει (*he shall inherit*).[175] The overcomer is said to inherit "ταῦτα" (*these*) which is a demonstrative pronoun—often rendered *these* or *those (things)*.[176] Since the adjective πάντα (**all**) is not in the Greek text—it is best to understand 'these things:'

> ...with reference to what follows, especially before clauses that express a statement, purpose, result, or condition, which it introduces.[177]

The Apostle John introduces the two specific '*things*' inherited by 'over-comers' through the particle καὶ. This particle is often used as a *coordinating conjunction*—but this is not the only grammatical

---

[173] Robinson, *Revelation 21:5*, GNT. Significantly, ποιῶ (make) is a 1st person singular verb I MAKE, which is further emphasized by the use of the 1st person singular pronoun Ἐγὼ 'I'.

[174] Danker, νικάω. Revelation 21:7, GNT, translation author.

[175] Thayer, κληρονομήσει. The New Testament consistently uses this word to denote an inheritance (*i.e. Matt. 5:5; Gal. 5:21; Heb. 1:4; 6:12 etc..*).

[176] Stevens, *Demonstrative Pronoun*. The KJV often supplies the word "things" for clarification (i.e. *'these things'* Luke 23:31; John 3:9; Acts 1:9 etc... or *'those things'* John 8:26; 29; Acts 17:11; 18:17 etc...).

[177] Danker, οὗτος.

function of καί.¹⁷⁸ In fact, Rev. 21:7 appears to use καί *explicatively* since it *"annexes epexegetically both words and sentences...so that it is equivalent to and indeed, namely..."*¹⁷⁹ This is not unusual, as καί is:

> often explicative; i.e. a word or clause is connected by means of καί with another word or clause, for the purpose of explaining what goes before it *and so, that is, namely.*¹⁸⁰

As an explicative—the particle '*spotlights*' the twofold promise given by the Alpha and Omega, which begins with: καί (*namely*) ἔσομαι αὐτῷ θεός (***I shall be God to [for] him***).¹⁸¹ It is important to note αὐτῷ is in the 'Dative' case; hence, the rendering *'to'* or *'for.'*¹⁸²

> The dative indicates *personal interest*. Often in Greek this is equivalent to the English *indirect object* ("to whom" or "for whom" something is done).¹⁸³

Thus, the first component of the twofold promise is that the Alpha and Omega will be θεός (God) *to* or *for* the overcomer.

John also uses the particle καί to introduce the second element of the promise given the overcomer saying: Καί (*namely*) αὐτὸς ἔσται μοι υἱός *(he shall be {my son} son of me).*¹⁸⁴ This declarative promise is often overlooked; yet, it provides revelatory insight concerning the **Divine identity** of the Alpha and Omega. This is especially true considering YHWH alone is identified as the 'Father' of Israel and of those who experience the New Birth.

> ...Blessed be thou, **LORD** (YHWH) God of Israel *our father, for ever and ever* (1Chronicles 29:10).
>
> Doubtless *thou art our father*...thou, O **LORD** (YHWH), art *our father*, our redeemer...(Isaiah 63:16).
>
> But now, O **LORD** (YHWH), thou *art our father*; we are the clay, and thou our potter; and we all are the work of thy hand

---

¹⁷⁸ A. T. Robertson, καί, (Greek Grammar). Electronic Edition. Robertson lists the *Adjunctive* use (also); *Ascensive* use (even); *Connective* use (and) as well as the *Epexegetic* or *Explicative* use.

¹⁷⁹ Thayer, καί. An explicative serves to unfold or explain or lay open an understanding.

¹⁸⁰ Danker, καί.

¹⁸¹ Robinson, GNT, with literal translation by the author.

¹⁸² Accordance Bible Software, *Revelation 21:7, Greek Parsing tool for GNT.*

¹⁸³ Stevens, *Greek Noun Components—Case.*

¹⁸⁴ Robinson, Rev. 21:7, GNT.

(Isaiah 64:8).

Have we not all **one father**? hath not one God created us?... (Malachi 2:10).

...come out from among them...and I will receive you, and will be a **Father** unto you, and ye shall be my sons and daughters, saith the **Lord Almighty** (2Corinthians 6:17-18).

Of further interest—the **one** 'Father' is designated as **the First** and **the Last**—a title that is also used of the <u>Alpha and Omega</u>, the glorified Messiah![185]

Thus saith the LORD (YHWH)...I am **the first** and I am **the last**; and beside me there is no God (Isaiah 44:6).

...I am he; I am **the first**, I also am **the last** (Isaiah 48:12).

And when I saw him, I fell at his feet as dead. And he laid his right hand upon me, saying unto me, Fear not; I am **the first** and **the last** (Revelation 1:17).

I am Alpha and Omega, the beginning and the end, **the first** and **the last** (Revelation 22:13).

The title <u>Alpha and Omega</u> is a Christological designator used exclusively in reference to the glorified Messiah—JESUS. Yet, the Apostle John identifies the <u>Alpha and Omega</u> as the First and the Last, which is a title used of the one true God—YHWH. Thus, Revelation 21:7 is an explicit testimony that the <u>Alpha and Omega</u> ultimately reveals HIMSELF to be the **one God and Father of the overcomer**! Unfortunately, the editorial omission of the '*red letters*' obscures the truth that Jesus is the visible incarnation of the one true God and Father—thereby perpetuating the current confusion that exists in Christendom concerning the identity of Jesus Christ.

Revelation 21:3-7 is a vivid portrayal of the day wherein the temporal gives way to the eternal and the mediatory ministry of the right hand place is abnegated. It is the day Jesus *plainly reveals* **HE** is *the visible personification of the One God and Father*. Yet, this passage also shows the close of the Messiah's session at the '*right hand*' does **not** mean the glorified Christ is obviated in eternity.

---

[185] Some might be inclined to think the reference to Yahweh as the <u>First</u> and the <u>Last</u> is the same a calling Him the Alpha and Omega. However, the Septuagint does **not** render Isaiah 44:6 or Isaiah 48:12 using the word **Αλφα** (Alpha) or <u>Ω</u> (Omega). Thus, there is no justification for suggesting a "person" other than JESUS is speaking in Revelation 21:5-7!

Scripture does not teach the '*person*' of Jesus is absorbed in or by the Deity—but that the redemptive mediatory function of 'the Son' is fulfilled in the eschaton. In fact, Jesus continues to be the *eternal tabernacle of God*—for the Father is permanently localized in the person and name of Jesus.

The word of God reveals that Yahweh's assumption of humanity carried *eternal consequences*. Indeed, through the incarnation—the **one true** God came to exist in a new way—as a <u>genuine human</u>, without encroaching on His existence as transcendent Spirit. In the fulness of time—God was visibly and permanently incarnate in '*the Son*' for the purpose of redemption. For thirty-three and a half years—the one true God **lived** as a <u>genuine human</u>; thus, he truly experienced <u>human birth at Bethlehem</u>, <u>human death on the cross</u>, <u>human burial</u>, <u>human resurrection</u>, and <u>human glorification</u> in the person of Jesus (1Timothy 3:16; 2Corinthians 5:19).

The incarnation is not a temporal theophany—but the <u>permanent incorporation of humanity</u> into God's identity through His tangible localization or personification in '*the Lamb.*' Thus, Jesus will ever be the *visible image* of the *invisible God*—insomuch that God's glory is ***eternally apprehended*** in the person and name JESUS!

> And I saw no temple therein: for the **Lord God Almighty** and **the Lamb** are the temple of it. And the city had no need of the sun, neither of the moon to shine in it; for **the glory of God** did lighten it, and the **Lamb is the light thereof** (Revelation 21:22-23).

The above verses affirm the permanency of God's incarnation in Jesus. At first glance, one may be inclined to think '<u>the Lord God Almighty</u>' and '<u>the Lamb</u>' refers to distinct entities. Yet, the Greek text explicitly reveals this is **one visible personage**—using the <u>third person singular verb</u> ἐστίν (**HE is**).[186] Indeed, the twenty second verse literally states the Lord God almighty and the lamb ναὸς αὐτῆς ἐστίν (*temple of it **HE IS**).[187]

The twenty-third verse gives further insight into this truth by emphasizing the eternal city has no need of the sun or moon—γὰρ

---
[186] Robinson, *Revelation 21:22*, GNT, parsing tool.
[187] Ibid., electronic Greek Interlinear.

δόξα *(for glory)* τοῦ θεοῦ *(of The God)* ἐφώτισεν αὐτήν *(he lightened it)*. The phrase *"glory of God:"*

> ...is often linked to dwelling (Hebrew *shajan*, **σκηνή**; Num 35:34; Ps 85:10 [sic] Sir 24:8; Ezek 43:7). In addition...the heavenly Jerusalem has within it the glory of God (his presence, his dwelling), and its brilliance is splendid like that of a precious stone (21:11). This divine glory illuminates the city...[188]

The Greek verb ἐφώτισεν signifies *"to function as a the source of light, to shine...to cause to be illumined, to give light to, light (up), illuminate."*[189] John identifies God's glory as the source of light in the city and that ὁ **λύχνος** αὐτῆς (*the lamp* of it) is τὸ ἀρνίον (*the lamb*). The KJV renders the phrase *"the lamb is the light thereof;"* yet, λύχνος actually refers to *"a hand-lamp, fed with oil"*[190] made of metal or clay![191] In fact, *"in some languages the closest equivalent of...λύχνος is a kerosene lamp.*[192]

The above information is important because it shows that God's glory is eternally '*encased in*' and '*emanating from*' the Lamb—the glorified Messiah—Jesus. This is a clear testimony that the person of the Son is **not** absorbed or eradicated in the eschaton—neither is he sitting or standing *on or at the right hand of God*. Rather, God's assumption of humanity in the incarnation is a perpetual witness to the cost of human redemption—for the one God and Father is eternally apprehended *in the singular person and name of Jesus*!

> And he shewed me a pure river of **water of life**, clear as cyrstal proceeding out of the **throne of God and of the Lamb**...And there shall be no more curse: but the **throne of God and of the Lamb** shall be in it; and **his** servants shall serve **him**: And they shall see **his** face; and **his** name *shall be* in their foreheads (Revelation 22:1, 3-4).

The above passage provides a final glimpse into the heavenly *"throne room,"* subsequent to the culmination of Psalm 110:1 and

---

[188] Spicq, δόξα. The 'glory of God' was previously examined. Also, the reference to Psalm 85:10 should be Psalm 85:9.

[189] Danker, φωτίζω.

[190] Richard Chenevix Trench, λύχνος, in Synonyms of the New Testament (Trench-Synonyms) electronic edition.

[191] Danker, λύχνος.

[192] Louw & Nida, λύχνος.

the revelatory disclosure of Rev. 21:3-7. The above passage begins with a reference to the *"water of life,"* promised to the overcomer by the <u>Alpha and Omega</u> (Rev. 21:6)! The significance of this final eschatological scene is that JESUS alone is seated **on the throne**! Indeed, like *every other verse* referencing God's throne—the word 'throne' θρόνου is **singular**—thus, there is <u>only one</u>!¹⁹³

Moreover, Revelation 21:3-7 reveals only **one personage** visibly occupies the throne. This is verified by the third person singular pronoun **αὐτός** (*he, him*)¹⁹⁴ which is used four times in verses three and four—in reference to the one seated on the throne!

> ...and **HIS** (αὐτοῦ) servants shall serve **HIM** (αὐτῷ) and they shall see **HIS** (αὐτοῦ) face and **HIS** (αὐτοῦ) name shall be in their foreheads (vrs. 3-4).¹⁹⁵

Equally important—Revelation 22:4 states the servants of the one seated on the throne have τὸ ὄνομα (*the name*) αὐτοῦ (*of him*). Like '*throne*'—τὸ ὄνομα '**the name**' is singular.¹⁹⁶ Thus, showing that HE that sits on the throne possesses **one singular name**! Yet, if there is only **one** <u>throne</u> and the **one** <u>occupying</u> the throne has only **one** <u>name</u>—why is it identified as τοῦ θρόνου (*the throne*) τοῦ θεοῦ (*of **the God***) καὶ τοῦ ἀρνίου (*and of **the Lamb**)?*¹⁹⁷

The answer to the above question begins with a <u>proper</u> grasp of the <u>soteriological-mediatory</u> significance of Jesus' '*session*' at '*the right hand*'—and its culmination in the eschaton. In addition, Revelation 22:1-4 can be correctly interpreted **only** by recognizing Jesus is the incarnation of the one God—**not** a hypostasis <u>of</u> or <u>in</u> God. Revelation 22:1-4 explicitly affirms the dual identity of Jesus as <u>genuinely human</u> and <u>THE God</u> manifest in flesh. Indeed, only one personage visibly seated on *"the throne of God and of the Lamb,"* accentuating the fact that <u>the Father</u> (YHWH) permanently united

---

¹⁹³ θρόνου, θρόνος, *Revelation 22: 1, 4,* <u>Greek New Testament</u> Parsing Tool.
¹⁹⁴ Gerald L. Stevens, *Pronouns.*
¹⁹⁵ Robinson, *Revelation 22:3-4,* <u>GNT</u>. This is also confirmed in Nestle-Aland, <u>Greek New Testament,</u> 27ᵗʰ edition (NA27-GBS), electronic edition.
¹⁹⁶ Robinson, *Revelation 22:4,* <u>GNT,</u> Greek-English interlinear.
¹⁹⁷ Ibid.

himself to humanity in the person and name of <u>the Son</u>—Jesus. Thus, eternity will reveal that JESUS is simultaneously our *'elder brother' (according to the flesh)* as well as the visible personification of YHWH—*'The mighty God'* and *'Everlasting Father.'*

Jesus is presently engaged in his mediatory work as high priest, which is symbolized by the metaphoric phrase *"the right hand of God."* Yet, Scripture teaches the *'right hand'* session is temporal and will culminate at the close of the human redemptive process. This is why Jesus is **never** seated at the right hand in the eschaton—but is the <u>**one**</u> seated on the throne! Indeed:

> The only God you will ever see is the Lord God whom John saw in the vision of the lampstands...The only God there is, is the great Father of us all. The one Lord God, Christ. In the Old Testament we call Him Jehovah. In the New Testament, the New Covenant, we call Him Jesus.[198]

---

[198] W. A. Criswell, <u>Expository Sermons on Revelation</u>, (Grand Rapids, MI: Zondervan, 1966), 146. Criswell affirms the doctrine of the Trinity; yet, his comments would raise the eyebrows of most Trinitarians.

## Selected Bibliography

Alford, Henry. The New Testament for English Readers. Vol. 1. Cambridge England, 1863.

Barnes, Albert. Notes on the Bible. Electronic format. Accordance Software 2010.

Berkhof, Louis. *States of Christ*. Summary of Christian Doctrine. Electronic edition, Accordance Software 2010.

Briggs, Charles A, Francis Brown and S.R. Driver. A Hebrew and English Lexicon of the Old Testament. Electronic edition. Oak Tree Software.

Brown, F.S.R. Driver and C.A. Briggs. Complete Brown-Driver-Briggs Hebrew and English Lexicon. Electronic Edition, 2010.

Broyles, Craig C. *The Redeeming King: Psalm 72's Contribution to the Messianic Ideal*. Studies in the Dead Sea Scrolls and Related Literature. Grand Rapids, MI: Eerdmans, 2005. Electronic.

Bruce, F. F. The Epistles to the Colossians to Philemon and to the Ephesians. The New International Commentary on the New Testament. Grand Rapids, MI: Eerdmans, 1984.

Bullinger, E. W. *Notes and Appendixes*. The Companion Bible. Grand Rapids, MI: Kregal, 1999.

Burton, Ernest De Witt. *Pure Final Clauses*. Syntax of the Moods and Tenses in New Testament Greek. Electronic edition.

Clarke, Adam. Adam Clarke Commentary. www.studylight.org.

Criswell, W. A. Expository Sermons on Revelation. Grand Rapids, MI: Zondervan, 1966.

Cullman, Oscar. Christology in the New Testament. Grand Rapids, MI: Baker, 1954.

Dahms, John V. *The Subordination of the Son*. Journal of the Evangelical Theological Society. 37/3. Louisville, KY: Evangelical Theological Society, September, 1994.

Dake, Finis Jennings. Dake's Annotated Reference Bible. Lawrenceville, GA, 1961.

Danker, Fredrick William. <u>A Greek-English Lexicon of the New Testament and other Early Christian Literature</u>. Third edition. Chicago, IL: University of Chicago, 2000. Electronic format.

Elliger, Karl and William Rudolph. Edts. <u>Biblia Hebraica Stuttgartensia</u>. Stuttgart, Germany: Deutsche Biblegesellschaft. Electronic edition. Accordance Software, 2010.

Eynikel, Lust, J.E. <u>A Greek-English Lexicon of the Septuagint</u>. Second edition. electronic format Accordance Software 2010.

Fee, Gordon D. <u>The First Epistle to the Corinthians</u>. <u>The New International Commentary on the New Testament</u>. Grand Rapids, MI: Eerdmans, 1997.

Flint, Peter W. Edt. <u>Studies in the Dead Sea Scrolls and Related Literature</u>. Grand Rapids, MI: Eerdmans. 2005. Electronic.

George, Timothy. <u>Galatians</u>. <u>The New American Commentary</u>. Vol. 30. Nashville, TN: Broadman & Holman, 1994.

Gill, John. <u>Gill's Exposition of the Entire Bible</u>. <u>www.bible.cc</u>.

Groves, J. Alan. <u>Groves-Wheeler Hebrew Morphology</u>. Glenside, PA: Center for Advanced Biblical Research, 2010. Electronic.

Grudem, Wayne. <u>Systematic Theology</u>. Grand Rapids, MI: Zondervan, 1994.

Harris, R. Laird. Edt. <u>Theological Wordbook of the Old Testament</u>. Electronic format. Accordance Software, 2010.

Hervey, A. C. <u>Acts & Romans</u>. Vol. 18. <u>The Pulpit Commentary</u>. Mclean, VA: McDonald.

Hodge, Charles. <u>Hodge's Systematic Theology</u>. Electronic Format. Accordance Software, 2010.

Jamieson, Robert., A. R. Fausset and David Brown. <u>Jamieson Fausset and Brown's Critical and Explanatory Commentary on the Whole Bible</u>. 1871 Edition, Woodside Bible Fellowship. Electronic format.

Jouon, Paul, S. J. & T. Muraoka. <u>A Grammar of Biblical Hebrew</u>. Rome, Italy: Editrice Pontifico Istituto Biblico, 2006.

Keil, C. F. and F. Delitzsch. Commentary on the Old Testament. 10 Vols. Peabody, MS: Hendrickson, reprint, 1996.

Koehler, Ludwig and Walter Baumgartner. The Hebrew and Aramaic Lexicon of the Old Testament. Leiden, Netherlands: Brill, 2000. Electronic edition.

Lewis, Scott. *So that God may be all in all*. Liber Annus. XL IX Jerusalem, Israel: Studium Biblicum Franciscanum, 1999.

Lindsay, James. The International Standard Bible Encyclopedia. www.topicalbible.org.

Louw, Johannes P. and Eugene A. Nida. Edts. Greek-English Lexicon of the New Testament Based on Semantic Domains. New York, NY: United Bible Societies, 1989. Electronic Format.

Marler, Stephen. Edt. Parsing Guide to the Greek Text of the KJV. Electronic edition.

Rahlfs, Alfred. Edt. Septuaginta. Stuttgart, Germany, 2006. Electronic edition, Accordance Software, 2010.

Robertson, A. T. Grammar of the Greek New Testament in the Light of Historical Research. Nashville, TN: Broadman, 1934.

_____. Robertson's Word Pictures. www.bibletools.org.

Robinson, Maurice A. and William G. Pierpont. The New Testament in the Orginal Greek: Byzantine Textform 2005.

Ross, Allen P. Introducing Biblical Hebrew. Electronic edition, 2001.

Stevens, Gerald L. New Testament Greek. Second edition, 1997. Electronic edition.

Strong, James. Strong's Hebrew and Chaldee Dictionary of the Old Testament. Electronic edition. Accordance Software, 2010.

Spicq, Ceslas. Theological Lexicon of the New Testament. Peabody, MA: Hendrickson, 1994. Electronic edition.

Trench, Richard Chenevix. Synonyms of the New Testament. Electronic edition.

VanGemeren, Willem A. Edt. New International Dictionary of Old Testament Theology and Exegesis. Grand Rapids, MI: Zondervan, 1997. Electronic edition.

Printed in Dunstable, United Kingdom